John Greenleaf Whittier

ONE HUNDRED BEST
AMERICAN POEMS

SELECTED BY

JOHN R. HOWARD

MANAGING EDITOR OF THE LIBRARY OF "THE
WORLD'S BEST POETRY"

NEW YORK
THOMAS Y. CROWELL COMPANY
PUBLISHERS

PREFACE

THIS grouping of American poems had its rise in the welcome accorded to a little volume entitled "The Hundred Best English Poems," issued by the same publishers. To select one hundred examples from the best work by our American poets, excluding all living authors, and avoiding an undue proportion of pieces by the few acknowledged to be preëminent, has been a puzzling although a pleasant task. Of course, no two editors would select the same hundred pieces from the sixty-four poets here represented. Any one familiar with our poetical literature will miss here certain favorites, and perhaps would criticize some of the selections. This is inevitable.

It is not always the most finished art which expresses feelings and "thoughts that shall live within the general mind." Many a simple poem has touched the popular heart by virtue of some genuine emotion or idea, melodiously if not artistically versified; and some of these will be found herein, because they have outlived their makers on the earth, and are still cherished for the pleasure, the consolation, or the spiritual uplift they afford. Yet, it may be added, there is hardly a piece in this little anthology that is not found in one or more of the larger collections made by critics of recognized taste, — such as Dana, Bryant, Stedman, and Warner. Thus a certain authoritative vote has been secured, which may give confidence in the result.

It is not claimed that these are The Hundred Best, but One Hundred from among the Best productions of our American poetical writers who have passed away. We begin with Philip Freneau (1752–1832), the pioneer among our American poets; and the list closes with the charming young writer, Richard Hovey, who died, too soon for his high promise, in 1900. The arrangement of the authors is in chronological order, —as nearly as that can be attained, — so that contrasts of style, changing with the times, may not be so discordantly apparent as is often observed with an alphabetical arrangement; but the index of authors, with titles of their poems, enables the reader easily to find any desired writer, and the index of first lines completes the simple finding-lists.

Some of the pieces of the later poets, being under copyright control, are printed here by the courteous consent of the owners; and thanks are rendered to the following houses and persons for permission to use poems by the authors named: Messrs. Little, Brown, & Co. for Emily Dickinson and Helen Hunt Jackson; The Lothrop Publishing Co. for Paul Hamilton Hayne; Messrs. Henry T. Coates & Co. for Mrs. Ethelinda E. Beers; the Neale Publishing Co. and Mrs. Mary M. B. Whitman for Henry Ames Blood; the J. B. Lippincott Co. for George H. Boker and Thomas Buchanan Read; Brentano's for John Henry Boner; the Robert Clarke Co. for General William Haines Lytle; Mr. P. J. Kenedy for Father Abram J. Ryan; and Messrs. Small, Maynard, & Co. for Walt Whitman and Richard Hovey. The poems thus permitted add much to the variety and the representative worth of the collection, and, it may be trusted, will induce readers to find fuller enjoyment in the volumes issued by those publishers, containing all the poems by the authors of whose work brief examples only are here given.

INDEX OF AUTHORS

ix

ONE HUNDRED BEST
AMERICAN POEMS

ONE HUNDRED BEST AMERICAN POEMS

PHILIP FRENEAU

The Wild Honeysuckle

FAIR flower, that dost so comely grow,
  Hid in this silent, dull retreat,
Untouched thy honied blossoms blow,
  Unseen thy little branches greet:
    No roving foot shall crush thee here,
    No busy hand provoke a tear.

By Nature's self in white arrayed,
  She bade thee shun the vulgar eye,
And planted here the guardian shade,
  And sent soft waters murmuring by;

Thus quietly thy summer goes,
Thy days declining to repose.

Smit with those charms that must decay,
   I grieve to see your future doom ;
They died — nor were those flowers more gay,
   The flowers that did in Eden bloom ;
      Unpitying frosts and Autumn's power
      Shall leave no vestige of this flower.

From morning suns and evening dews
   At first thy little being came ;
If nothing once, you nothing lose,
   For when you die you are the same ;
      The space between is but an hour,
      The frail duration of a flower.

TIMOTHY DWIGHT

2 *Columbia*

COLUMBIA, Columbia, to glory arise,
The queen of the world and the child of the
    skies!
Thy genius commands thee; with rapture be-
    hold,
While ages on ages thy splendors unfold.
Thy reign is the last and the noblest of time,
Most fruitful thy soil, most inviting thy clime;
Let the crimes of the East ne'er encrimson thy
    name,
Be freedom and science and virtue thy fame.

To conquest and slaughter let Europe aspire;
Whelm nations in blood, and wrap cities in fire;
Thy heroes the rights of mankind shall defend,
And triumph pursue them, and glory attend.
A world is thy realm; for a world be thy laws
Enlarged as thine empire, and just as thy cause;

On Freedom's broad basis that empire shall
    rise,
Extend with the main, and dissolve with the
    skies,

Fair Science her gates to thy sons shall unbar,
And the East see thy morn hide the beams of
    her star;
New bards and new sages unrivalled shall soar
To fame unextinguished when time is no more;
To thee, the last refuge of virtue designed,
Shall fly from all nations the best of mankind;
Here, grateful to Heaven, with transport shall
    bring
Their incense, more fragrant than odors of
    spring.

Nor less shall thy fair ones to glory ascend,
And genius and beauty in harmony blend;
The graces of form shall awake pure desire,
And the charms of the soul ever cherish the
    fire;
Their sweetness unmingled, their manners
    refined,

And virtue's bright image enstamped on the
    mind,
With peace and soft rapture shall teach life to
    glow,
And light up a smile on the aspect of woe.

Thy fleets to all regions thy power shall display,
The nations admire, and the ocean obey;
Each shore to thy glory its tribute unfold,
And the East and the South yield their spices
    and gold.
As the dayspring unbounded thy splendor shall
    flow,
And earth's little kingdoms before thee shall
    bow,
While the ensigns of union, in triumph unfurled,
Hush the tumult of war, and give peace to the
    world.

Thus, as down a lone valley, with cedars o'er-
    spread,
From war's dread confusion, I pensively
    strayed, —

The gloom from the face of fair heaven retired;
The wind ceased to murmur, the thunders expired;
Perfumes, as of Eden, flowed sweetly along,
And a voice, as of angels, enchantingly sung:
"Columbia, Columbia, to glory arise,
The queen of the world, and the child of the skies!"

FRANCIS SCOTT KEY

3

The Star-spangled Banner

O say, can you see, by the dawn's early light,
  What so proudly we hailed at the twilight's
    last gleaming, —
Whose broad stripes and bright stars, through
    the perilous fight
  O'er the ramparts we watched, were so gal-
    lantly streaming!
And the rocket's red glare, the bombs bursting
    in air,
Gave proof through the night that our flag was
    still there;
O! say, does that star-spangled banner yet
    wave
O'er the land of the free, and the home of the
    brave?

On that shore dimly seen through the mists of
    the deep,

Where the foe's haughty host in dread silence
    reposes,
What is that which the breeze, o'er the towering
    steep,
    As it fitfully blows, now conceals, now dis-
        closes?
Now it catches the gleam of the morning's first
    beam,
In full glory reflected now shines on the stream;
'Tis the star-spangled banner; O long may it
    wave
O'er the land of the free, and the home of the
    brave!

And where is that band who so vauntingly
    swore
    That the havoc of war and the battle's con-
        fusion
A home and a country should leave us no
    more?
    Their blood has washed out their foul foot-
        steps' pollution.
No refuge could save the hireling and slave

From the terror of flight, or the gloom of the
   grave;
And the star-spangled banner in triumph doth
   wave
O'er the land of the free, and the home of the
   brave.

O! thus be it ever, when freemen shall stand
   Between their loved homes and the war's
   desolation!
Blest with vict'ry and peace, may the Heav'n-
   rescued land
   Praise the power that hath made and pre-
   served us a nation.
Then conquer we must, when our cause it is
   just,
And this be our motto — "*In God is our trust.*"
And the star-spangled banner in triumph shall
   wave
O'er the land of the free, and the home of the
   brave.

CLEMENT CLARKE MOORE

4

A Visit from St. Nicholas

'TWAS the night before Christmas, when all
    through the house
Not a creature was stirring, not even a mouse;
The stockings were hung by the chimney with
    care,
In hopes that St. Nicholas soon would be there;
The children were nestled all snug in their
    beds,
While visions of sugar-plums danced in their
    heads;
And mamma in her 'kerchief, and I in my cap,
Had just settled our brains for a long winter's
    nap, —
When out on the lawn there arose such a
    clatter,
I sprang from my bed to see what was the
    matter.

Away to the window I flew like a flash,
Tore open the shutters and threw up the sash.
The moon on the breast of the new-fallen snow
Gave a lustre of mid-day to objects below ;
When what to my wondering eyes should ap-
    pear,
But a miniature sleigh and eight tiny reindeer,
With a little old driver, so lively and quick
I knew in a moment it must be St. Nick.
More rapid than eagles his coursers they came,
And he whistled and shouted, and called them
    by name :
" Now, *Dasher!* now, *Dancer!* now, *Prancer*
    and *Vixen!*
On, *Comet!* on, *Cupid!* on, *Donder* and *Blitzen!*
To the top of the porch, to the top of the wall !
Now dash away, dash away, dash away all ! "
As dry leaves that before the wild hurricane fly,
When they meet with an obstacle, mount to the
    sky,
So up to the house-top the coursers they flew,
With the sleigh full of toys, — and St. Nicholas
    too.

And then in a twinkling I heard on the roof
The prancing and pawing of each little hoof.
As I drew in my head, and was turning
    around,
Down the chimney St. Nicholas came with a
    bound.
He was dressed all in fur from his head to his
    foot,
And his clothes were all tarnished with ashes
    and soot;
A bundle of toys he had flung on his back,
And he looked like a pedler just opening his
    pack.
His eyes how they twinkled! his dimples how
    merry!
His cheeks were like roses, his nose like a
    cherry;
His droll little mouth was drawn up like a bow,
And the beard on his chin was as white as the
    snow;
The stump of a pipe he held tight in his teeth,
And the smoke it encircled his head like a
    wreath;

He had a broad face and a little round belly
That shook, when he laughed, like a bowl full
    of jelly.
He was chubby and plump, — a right jolly old
    elf,
And I laughed, when I saw him, in spite of
    myself;
A wink of his eye and a twist of his head
Soon gave me to know I had nothing to dread;
He spoke not a word, but went straight to his
    work,
And filled all the stockings; then turned with
    a jerk,
And laying his finger aside of his nose,
And giving a nod, up the chimney he rose;
He sprang to his sleigh, to his team gave a
    whistle,
And away they all flew like the down of a
    thistle.
But I heard him exclaim, ere he drove out of
    sight,
"*Happy Christmas to all, and to all a good
    night!*"

SAMUEL WOODWORTH

5

The Bucket

How dear to this heart are the scenes of my
    childhood,
  When fond recollection presents them to
    view !
The orchard, the meadow, the deep-tangled wild-
    wood,
  And every loved spot which my infancy
    knew !
The wide-spreading pond, and the mill that
    stood by it,
  The bridge, and the rock where the cataract
    fell,
The cot of my father, the dairy-house nigh it ;
  And e'en the rude bucket that hung in the
    well —
The old oaken bucket, the iron-bound bucket,
The moss-covered bucket which hung in the
    well.

That moss-covered vessel I hailed as a treasure,
    For often at noon, when returned from the
       field,
I found it the source of an exquisite pleasure,
    The purest and sweetest that nature can
       yield,
How ardent I seized it, with hands that were
       glowing,
    And quick to the white-pebbled bottom it
       fell;
Then soon, with the emblem of truth over-
       flowing,
    And dripping with coolness, it rose from the
       well —
The old oaken bucket, the iron-bound bucket,
The moss-covered bucket arose from the well.

How sweet from the green, mossy brim to
       receive it,
    As poised on the curb it inclined to my lips!
Not a full, blushing goblet could tempt me to
       leave it,
    The brightest that beauty or revelry sips.

And now, far removed from the loved habita.
    tion,
   The tear of regret will intrusively swell,
As fancy reverts to my father's plantation,
   And sighs for the bucket that hangs in the
      well —
The old oaken bucket, the iron-bound bucket,
The moss-covered bucket that hangs in the
   well!

JOHN PIERPONT

6   *The Pilgrim Fathers*

THE Pilgrim Fathers — where are they?
  The waves that brought them o'er
Still roll in the bay, and throw their spray
  As they break along the shore;
Still roll in the bay, as they rolled that day
  When the *Mayflower* moored below,
When the sea around was black with storms,
  And white the shore with snow.

The mists, that wrapped the Pilgrim's sleep,
  Still brood upon the tide;
And the rocks yet keep their watch by the deep
  To stay its waves of pride.
But the snow-white sail, that he gave to the gale,
  When the heavens looked dark, is gone, —
As an angel's wing through an opening cloud
  Is seen, and then withdrawn.

The Pilgrim exile — sainted name!
  The hill whose icy brow
Rejoiced, when he came, in the morning's flame,
  In the morning's flame burns now.
And the moon's cold light, as it lay that night
  On the hillside and the sea,
Still lies where he laid his houseless head, —
  But the Pilgrim! where is he?

The Pilgrim Fathers are at rest:
  When summer is throned on high,
And the world's warm breast is in verdure drest,
  Go, stand on the hill where they lie.
The earliest ray of the golden day,
  On that hallowed spot is cast;
And the evening sun, as he leaves the world,
  Looks kindly on that spot last.

The Pilgrim spirit has not fled:
  It walks in noon's broad light;
And it watches the bed of the glorious dead,
  With the holy stars by night.

It watches the bed of the brave who have bled,
    And still guard this ice-bound shore,
Till the waves of the bay, where the *Mayflower*
    lay,
    Shall foam and freeze no more.

RICHARD HENRY DANA

7   *The Little Beach-bird*

Thou little bird, thou dweller by the sea,
  Why takest thou its melancholy voice,
    And with that boding cry
    Why o'er the waves dost fly?
O, rather, bird, with me
  Through the fair land rejoice!

Thy flitting form comes ghostly dim and pale,
  As driven by a beating storm at sea;
    Thy cry is weak and scared,
    As if thy mates had shared
The doom of us: thy wail, —
  What doth it bring to me?

Thou call'st along the sand, and haunt'st the
        surge,
  Restless and sad; as if, in strange accord
    With the motion and the roar
    Of waves that drive to shore,

One spirit did ye urge —
   The Mystery — the Word.

Of thousands, thou, both sepulchre and pall,
   Old Ocean! A requiem o'er the dead
      From out thy gloomy cells
      A tale of mourning tells, —
Tells of man's woe and fall,
   His sinless glory fled.

Then turn thee, little bird, and take thy flight
   Where the complaining sea shall sadness
      bring
      Thy spirit never more;
      Come, quit with me the shore,
And on the meadows light
   Where birds for gladness sing!

RICHARD HENRY WILD

To the Mocking-bird

WINGED mimic of the woods! thou motley fool!
Who shall thy gay buffoonery describe?
Thine ever ready notes of ridicule
Pursue thy fellows still with jest and gibe.
Wit, sophist, songster, Yorick of thy tribe,
Thou sportive satirist of Nature's school,
To thee the palm of scoffing we ascribe,
Arch-mocker and mad Abbot of Misrule!
For such thou art by day — but all night long
Thou pourest a soft, sweet, pensive, solemn
      strain,
As if thou didst in this thy moonlight song
Like to the melancholy Jacques complain,
Musing on falsehood, folly, vice, and wrong,
And sighing for thy motley coat again.

JOHN GARDINER CALKINS
BRAINARD

9   *The Fall of Niagara*

THE thoughts are strange that crowd into my
     brain,
While I look upward to thee. It would seem
As if God poured thee from his hollow hand,
And hung his bow upon thine awful front,
And spoke in that loud voice which seemed to
     him
Who dwelt in Patmos for his Saviour's sake
The sound of many waters; and had bade
Thy flood to chronicle the ages back,
And notch his centuries in the eternal rocks.

     Deep calleth unto deep. And what are we,
That hear the question of that voice sublime?
O, what are all the notes that ever rung
From war's vain trumpet, by thy thundering
     side?

Yea, what is all the riot man can make
In his short life, to thy unceasing roar?
And yet, bold babbler, what art thou to Him
Who drowned a world, and heaped the waters
    far
Above its loftiest mountains? — a light wave
That breaks, and whispers of its Maker's might.

JOSEPH RODMAN DRAKE

10 *The American Flag*

WHEN Freedom, from her mountain height
   Unfurled her standard to the air,
She tore the azure robe of night,
   And set the stars of glory there!
She mingled with its gorgeous dyes
The milky baldric of the skies,
And striped its pure, celestial white
With streakings of the morning light;
Then, from his mansion in the sun,
She called her eagle-bearer down,
And gave into his mighty hand
The symbol of her chosen land.

Majestic monarch of the cloud!
   Who rear'st aloft thy regal form,
To hear the tempest trumpings loud,
And see the lightning lances driven,
   When strive the warriors of the storm,

And rolls the thunder-drum of heaven, —
Child of the sun! to thee 'tis given
  To guard the banner of the free,
To hover in the sulphur smoke,
To ward away the battle stroke,
And bid its blendings shine afar,
Like rainbows on the cloud of war,
  The harbingers of victory!

Flag of the brave! thy folds shall fly
The sign of hope and triumph high!
When speaks the signal trumpet tone,
And the long line comes gleaming on,
Ere yet the life-blood, warm and wet,
Has dimmed the glistening bayonet,
Each soldier eye shall brightly turn
To where thy sky-born glories burn,
And, as his springing steps advance,
Catch war and vengeance from the glance.
And when the cannon-mouthings loud
Heave in wild wreaths the battle shroud
And gory sabres rise and fall
Like shoots of flame on midnight's pall,

Then shall thy meteor glances glow,
  And cowering foes shall sink beneath
Each gallant arm that strikes below
  That lovely messenger of death.

Flag of the seas! on ocean wave
Thy stars shall glitter o'er the brave;
When death, careering on the gale,
Sweeps darkly round the bellied sail,
And frighted waves rush wildly back
Before the broadside's reeling rack,
Each dying wanderer of the sea
Shall look at once to heaven and thee,
And smile to see thy splendors fly
In triumph o'er his closing eye.

Flag of the free heart's hope and home,
  By angel hands to valor given!
Thy stars have lit the welkin dome,
  And all thy hues were born in heaven.
Forever float that standard sheet!
  Where breathes the foe but falls before us,

With Freedom's soil beneath our feet,
    And Freedom's banner streaming o'er us ![1]

II   *The Culprit Fay*

> " My visual orbs are purged from film, and, lo !
>   Instead of Anster's turnip-bearing vales,
>   I see old fairy-land's miraculous show !
>   Her trees of tinsel kissed by freakish gales,
>   Her ouphes that, cloaked in leaf-gold, skim the breeze,
>   And fairies, swarming . . ."
>   TENNANT'S *Anster Fair.*

'Tis the middle watch of a summer's night, —
The earth is dark, but the heavens are bright ;
Naught is seen in the vault on high
But the moon, and the stars, and the cloudless
    sky,
And the flood which rolls its milky hue,
A river of light on the welkin blue.

---

[1] The last four lines are by Halleck. Those originally written
by Drake were thus : —

> "And fixed as yonder orb divine,
>   That saw thy bannered blaze unfurled,
>   Shall thy proud stars resplendent shine,
>   The guard and glory of the world."

The moon looks down on old Cro'nest;
She mellows the shades on his shaggy breast,
And seems his huge gray form to throw
In a silver cone on the wave below.
His sides are broken by spots of shade,
By the walnut bough and the cedar made;
And through their clustering branches dark
Glimmers and dies the firefly's spark, —
Like starry twinkles that momently break
Through the rifts of the gathering tempest's
    rack.

The stars are on the moving stream,
    And fling, as its ripples gently flow,
A burnished length of wavy beam
    In an eel-like, spiral line below;
The winds are whist, and the owl is still;
    The bat in the shelvy rock is hid;
And naught is heard on the lonely hill
But the cricket's chirp, and the answer shrill
    Of the gauze-winged katydid;
And the plaint of the wailing whippoorwill,
    Who moans unseen, and ceaseless sings

Ever a note of wail and woe,
  Till morning spreads her rosy wings,
And earth and sky in her glances glow.

'Tis the hour of fairy ban and spell:
The wood-tick has kept the minutes well;
He has counted them all with click and stroke
Deep in the heart of the mountain-oak,
And he has awakened the sentry elve
  Who sleeps with him in the haunted tree,
To bid him ring the hour of twelve,
  And calls the fays to their revelry;
Twelve small strokes on his tinkling bell
('Twas made of the white snail's pearly shell).
"Midnight comes, and all is well!
Hither, hither wing your way!
'Tis the dawn of the fairy-day."
They come from beds of lichen green,
They creep from the mullein's velvet screen;
  Some on the backs of beetles fly
From the silver tops of moon-touched trees,
  Where they swung in their cobweb hammocks
    high,

And rocked about in the evening breeze;
  Some from the hum-bird's downy nest, —
They had driven him out by elfin power,
  And, pillowed on plumes of his rainbow
      breast,
Had slumbered there till the charmèd hour;
  Some had lain in the scoop of the rock,
With glittering ising-stars inlaid;
  And some had opened the four-o'clock,
And stole within its purple shade.

  And now they throng the moonlight glade,
Above, below, on every side, —
  Their little minim forms arrayed
In the tricksy pomp of fairy pride!

They come not now to print the lea,
In freak and dance around the tree,
Or at the mushroom board to sup,
And drink the dew from the buttercup:
A scene of sorrow waits them now,
For an ouphe has broken his vestal vow;
He has loved an earthly maid,
And left for her his woodland shade;

He has lain upon her lip of dew,
And sunned him in her eye of blue,
Fanned her cheek with his wing of air,
Played in the ringlets of her hair,
And, nestling on her snowy breast,
Forgot the lily-king's behest.
For this the shadowy tribes of air
    To the elfin court must haste away:
And now they stand expectant there,
    To hear the doom of the culprit fay.[1]

---

[1] It is impracticable in our limited space to give the whole of this exquisite piece of fancy, written by Drake (within three days) to prove to Halleck, Cooper, and DeKay that American rivers might be made as romantic as the streams celebrated in Scottish poetry. The flavor of it, however, appears in the introductory stanzas here printed.

FITZ-GREENE HALLECK

On the Death of Joseph Rodman Drake

GREEN be the turf above thee,
　　Friend of my better days!
None knew thee but to love thee,
　　Nor named thee but to praise.

Tears fell, when thou wert dying,
　　From eyes unused to weep,
And long where thou art lying,
　　Will tears the cold turf steep.

When hearts whose truth was proven,
　　Like thine, are laid in earth,
There should a wreath be woven
　　To tell the world their worth;

And I, who woke each morrow
　　To clasp thy hand in mine,
Who shared thy joy and sorrow,
　　Whose weal and woe were thine;

It should be mine to braid it
    Around thy faded brow,
But I've in vain essayed it,
    And feel I cannot now.

While memory bid me weep thee,
    Nor thoughts nor words are free,
The grief is fixed too deeply
    That mourns a man like thee.

13   *Marco Bozzaris*

AT midnight, in his guarded tent,
    The Turk was dreaming of the hour
When Greece, her knee in suppliance bent,
    Should tremble at his power:
In dreams, through camp and court he bore
The trophies of a conqueror;
    In dreams his song of triumph heard;
Then wore his monarch's signet ring:
Then pressed that monarch's throne—a king;
As wild his thoughts, and gay of wing,
    As Eden's garden bird.

At midnight, in the forest shades,
    Bozzaris ranged his Suliote band,
True as the steel of their tried blades,
    Heroes in heart and hand.
There had the Persian's thousands stood,
There had the glad earth drunk their blood
    On old Platæa's day;
And now there breathed that haunted air
The sons of sires who conquered there,
With arm to strike, and soul to dare,
    As quick, as far as they.

An hour passed on — the Turk awoke;
    That bright dream was his last;
He woke — to hear his sentries shriek,
    "To arms! they come! the Greek! the
        Greek!"
He woke — to die midst flame, and smoke,
And shout, and groan, and sabre-stroke,
    And death-shots falling thick and fast
As lightnings from the mountain-cloud;
And heard, with voice as trumpet loud,
    Bozzaris cheer his band.

" Strike — till the last armed foe expires ;
Strike — for your altars and your fires ;
Strike — for the green graves of your sires,
   GOD, and your native land ! "

They fought — like brave men, long and well ;
   They piled that ground with Moslem slain ;
They conquered — but Bozzaris fell,
   Bleeding at every vein.
His few surviving comrades saw
His smile when rang their proud hurrah,
   And the red field was won ;
Then saw in death his eyelids close
Calmly, as to a night's repose,
   Like flowers at set of sun.

Come to the bridal chamber, Death !
   Come to the mother's, when she feels,
For the first time, her first-born's breath ;
   Come when the blessèd seals
That close the pestilence are broke,
And crowded cities wail its stroke ;
Come in consumption's ghastly form,
The earthquake shock, the ocean storm ;

Come when the heart beats high and warm,
  With banquet-song, and dance, and wine;
And thou art terrible — the tear,
The groan, the knell, the pall, the bier,
And all we know, or dream, or fear
  Of agony, are thine.

But to the hero, when his sword
  Has won the battle for the free,
Thy voice sounds like a prophet's word;
And in its hollow tones are heard
  The thanks of millions yet to be.
Come, when his task of fame is wrought —
Come with her laurel-leaf, blood-bought —
  Come in her crowning hour — and then
Thy sunken eye's unearthly light
To him is welcome as the sight
  Of sky and stars to prisoned men;
Thy grasp is welcome as the hand
Of brother in a foreign land;
Thy summons welcome as the cry
That told the Indian isles were nigh
  To the world-seeking Genoese,

When the land-wind, from woods of palm,
And orange-groves, and fields of balm,
   Blew o'er the Haytian seas.

Bozzaris! with the storied brave
   Greece nurtured in her glory's time,
Rest thee — there is no prouder grave,
   Even in her own proud clime.
She wore no funeral weeds for thee,
   Nor bade the dark hearse wave its plume,
Like torn branch of death's leafless tree,
In sorrow's pomp and pageantry,
   The heartless luxury of the tomb:
But she remembers thee as one
Long loved and for a season gone.
For thee her poet's lyre is wreathed,
Her marble wrought, her music breathed;
For thee she rings the birthday bells;
Of thee her babes' first lisping tells;
For thine her evening prayer is said
At palace couch, and cottage bed;
Her soldier, closing with the foe,
Gives for thy sake a deadlier blow;

His plighted maiden, when she fears
For him, the joy of her young years,
Thinks of thy fate, and checks her tears;
    And she, the mother of thy boys,
Though in her eye and faded cheek
Is read the grief she will not speak,
    The memory of her buried joys,
And even she who gave thee birth,
Will, by their pilgrim-circled hearth,
    Talk of thy doom without a sigh;
For thou art Freedom's now, and Fame's:
One of the few, the immortal names,
    That were not born to die.

CHARLES SPRAGUE

14   *The Winged Worshippers* [1]

GAY, guiltless pair,
What seek ye from the fields of heaven?
Ye have no need of prayer,
Ye have no sins to be forgiven.

Why perch ye here,
Where mortals to their Maker bend?
Can your pure spirits fear
The God ye never could offend?

Ye never knew
The crimes for which we come to weep.
Penance is not for you,
Blessed wanderers of the upper deep.

To you 'tis given
To wake sweet Nature's untaught lays;

[1] " Addressed to two swallows that flew into the Chauncey Place church during divine service."

Beneath the arch of heaven
To chirp away a life of praise.

Then spread each wing,
Far, far above, o'er lakes and lands,
And join the choirs that sing
In yon blue dome not reared with hands

Or, if ye stay,
To note the consecrated hour,
Teach me the airy way,
And let me try your envied power.

Above the crowd,
On upward wings could I but fly,
I'd bathe in yon bright cloud,
And seek the stars that gem the sky.

'Twere Heaven indeed
Through fields of trackless light to soar,
On Nature's charms to feed,
And Nature's own great God adore.

JAMES GATES PERCIVAL

The Coral Grove

DEEP in the wave is a coral grove,
Where the purple mullet and goldfish rove,
Where the sea-flower spreads its leaves of blue,
That never are wet with falling dew,
But in bright and changeful beauty shine,
Far down in the green and glassy brine.
The floor is of sand like the mountain drift,
And the pearl-shells spangle the flinty snow;
From coral rocks the sea-plants lift
Their boughs, where the tides and billows flow;
The water is calm and still below,
For the winds and waves are absent there,
And the sands are bright as the stars that glow
In the motionless fields of upper air:
There with its waving blade of green,
The sea-flag streams through the silent water,
And the crimson leaf of the dulse is seen
To blush, like a banner bathed in slaughter:

There with a light and easy motion,
The fan-coral sweeps through the clear, deep
     sea;
And the yellow and scarlet tufts of ocean
Are bending like corn on the upland lea:
And life, in rare and beautiful forms,
Is sporting amid those bowers of stone,
And is safe, when the wrathful Spirit of storms
Has made the top of the wave his own:
And when the ship from his fury flies,
Where the myriad voices of Ocean roar,
When the wind-god frowns in the murky skies,
And demons are waiting the wreck on shore;
Then far below, in the peaceful sea,
The purple mullet and gold-fish rove,
Where the waters murmur tranquilly,
Through the bending twigs of the coral grove.

16   *Thanatopsis*

To him who in the love of Nature holds
Communion with her visible forms, she speaks
A various language; for his gayer hours
She has a voice of gladness, and a smile
And eloquence of beauty, and she glides
Into his darker musings, with a mild
And healing sympathy, that steals away
Their sharpness, ere he is aware.   When thoughts
Of the last bitter hour come like a blight
Over thy spirit, and sad images
Of the stern agony, and shroud, and pall,
And breathless darkness, and the narrow house,
Make thee to shudder, and grow sick at heart;—
Go forth, under the open sky, and list
To Nature's teachings, while from all around—
Earth and her waters, and the depths of air —
Comes a still voice:—Yet a few days, and thee

The all-beholding sun shall see no more
In all his course; nor yet in the cold ground,
Where thy pale form was laid, with many tears,
Nor in the embrace of ocean, shall exist
Thy image. Earth, that nourished thee, shall
    claim
Thy growth, to be resolved to earth again,
And, lost each human trace, surrendering up
Thine individual being, shalt thou go
To mix forever with the elements,
To be a brother to the insensible rock
And to the sluggish clod, which the rude swain
Turns with his share, and treads upon. The
    oak
Shall send his roots abroad, and pierce thy
    mould.

    Yet not to thine eternal resting-place
Shalt thou retire alone — nor couldst thou wish
Couch more magnificent. Thou shalt lie down
With patriarchs of the infant world — with
    kings,
The powerful of the earth — the wise, the good,
Fair forms, and hoary seers of ages past,

All in one mighty sepulchre. — The hills,
Rock-ribbed, and ancient as the sun, — the vales
Stretching in pensive quietness between;
The venerable woods — rivers that move
In majesty, and the complaining brooks
That make the meadows green; and, poured
    round all,
Old ocean's gray and melancholy waste, —
Are but the solemn decorations all
Of the great tomb of man.   The golden sun,
The planets, all the infinite host of heaven,
Are shining on the sad abodes of death,
Through the still lapse of ages.   All that tread
The globe are but a handful to the tribes
That slumber in its bosom. — Take the wings
Of morning, and the Barcan desert pierce,
Or lose thyself in the continuous woods
Where rolls the Oregan, and hears no sound
Save his own dashings — yet — the dead are
    there;
And millions in those solitudes, since first
The flight of years began, have laid them down
In their last sleep — the dead reign there alone.

So shalt thou rest — and what if thou withdraw
Unheeded by the living — and no friend
Take note of thy departure? All that breathe
Will share thy destiny. The gay will laugh
When thou art gone, the solemn brood of care
Plod on, and each one as before will chase
His favorite phantom; yet all these shall leave
Their mirth and their employments, and shall
    come
And make their bed with thee. As the long
    train
Of ages glide away, the sons of men,
The youth in life's green spring, and he who
    goes
In the full strength of years, matron, and maid,
And the sweet babe, and the gray-headed
    man, —
Shall one by one be gathered to thy side,
By those who in their turn shall follow them.

So live, that when thy summons comes to
    join
The innumerable caravan, that moves

To that mysterious realm, where each shall take
His chamber in the silent halls of death,
Thou go not, like the quarry-slave at night,
Scourged to his dungeon, but, sustained and
    soothed
By an unfaltering trust, approach thy grave
Like one who wraps the drapery of his couch
About him, and lies down to pleasant dreams.

17   *The Crowded Street*

LET me move slowly through the street,
    Filled with an ever-shifting train,
Amid the sound of steps that beat
    The murmuring walks like autumn rain.

How fast the flitting figures come!
    The mild, the fierce, the stony face;
Some bright with thoughtless smiles, and some
    Where secret tears have left their trace.

They pass — to toil, to strife, to rest;
    To halls in which the feast is spread;

To chambers where the funeral guest
  In silence sits beside the dead.

And some to happy homes repair,
  Where children, pressing cheek to cheek,
With mute caresses shall declare
  The tenderness they cannot speak.

And some, who walk in calmness here,
  Shall shudder as they reach the door
Where one who made their dwelling dear,
  Its flower, its light, is seen no more.

Youth, with pale cheek and slender frame,
  And dreams of greatness in thine eye!
Goest thou to build an early name,
  Or early in the task to die?

Keen son of trade, with eager brow!
  Who is now fluttering in thy snare?
Thy golden fortunes, tower they now,
  Or melt the glittering spires in air?

Who of this crowd to-night shall tread
  The dance till daylight gleam again?

Who sorrow o'er the untimely dead?
  Who writhe in throes of mortal pain?

Some, famine-struck, shall think how long
  The cold dark hours, how slow the light!
And some, who flaunt amid the throng,
  Shall hide in dens of shame to-night.

Each, where his tasks or pleasures call,
  They pass, and heed each other not.
There is who heeds, who holds them all,
  In His large love and boundless thought.

These struggling tides of life that seem
  In wayward, aimless course to tend,
Are eddies of the mighty stream
  That rolls to its appointed end.

18   *The Death of the Flowers*

THE melancholy days are come, the saddest of
    the year,
Of wailing winds, and naked woods, and mead-
    ows brown and sear.

Heaped in the hollows of the grove, the with-
    ered leaves lie dead;
They rustle to the eddying gust, and to the
    rabbit's tread.
The robin and the wren are flown, and from
    the shrubs the jay,
And from the wood-top calls the crow, through
    all the gloomy day.

Where are the flowers, the fair young flowers,
    that lately sprang and stood
In brighter light and softer airs, a beauteous
    sisterhood?
Alas! they all are in their graves, the gentle
    race of flowers
Are lying in their lowly beds, with the fair and
    good of ours.
The rain is falling where they lie, but the cold
    November rain,
Calls not, from out the gloomy earth, the lovely
    ones again.

The wind-flower and the violet, they perished
    long ago,

And the brier-rose and the orchis died amid
    the summer glow;
But on the hill the golden-rod, and the aster
    in the wood,
And the yellow sun-flower by the brook in
    autumn beauty stood,
Till fell the frost from the clear cold heaven,
    as falls the plague on men,
And the brightness of their smile was gone,
    from upland, glade, and glen.

And now, when comes the calm mild day, as
    still such days will come,
To call the squirrel and the bee from out their
    winter home;
When the sound of dropping nuts is heard,
    though all the trees are still,
And twinkle in the smoky light the waters of
    the rill,
The south wind searches for the flowers whose
    fragrance late he bore,
And sighs to find them in the wood and by the
    stream no more.

And then I think of one who in her youthful
  beauty died,
The fair, meek blossom that grew up and faded
  by my side;
In the cold moist earth we laid her, when the
  forest cast the leaf,
And we wept that one so lovely should have a
  life so brief:
Yet not unmeet it was that one, like that young
  friend of ours,
So gentle and so beautiful, should perish with
  the flowers.

19   *To a Waterfowl*

  WHITHER, 'midst falling dew,
While glow the heavens with the last steps of
  day,
Far, through their rosy depths, dost thou
  pursue
      Thy solitary way?

    Vainly the fowler's eye
Might mark thy distant flight to do thee wrong,

As, darkly painted on the crimson sky,
    Thy figure floats along.

        Seek'st thou the plashy brink
Of weedy lake, or marge of river wide,
Or where the rocking billows rise and sink
        On the chafed ocean side?

        There is a Power whose care
Teaches thy way along that pathless coast,
The desert and illimitable air —
        Lone wandering, but not lost.

        All day thy wings have fanned,
At that far height, the cold thin atmosphere,
Yet stoop not, weary, to the welcome land,
        Though the dark night is near,

        And soon that toil shall end;
Soon shalt thou find a summer home, and rest,
And scream among thy fellows; reeds shall
    bend,
        Soon, o'er thy sheltered nest.

        Thou'rt gone, the abyss of heaven
Hath swallowed up thy form; yet, on my heart

Deeply hath sunk the lesson thou hast given,
    And shall not soon depart.

He who, from zone to zone,
Guides through the boundless sky thy certain
    flight,
In the long way that I must tread alone
    Will lead my steps aright.

20   *To the Fringed Gentian*

Thou blossom bright with autumn dew,
And colored with the heaven's own blue,
That openest, when the quiet light
Succeeds the keen and frosty night.

Thou comest not when violets lean
O'er wandering brooks and springs unseen,
Or columbines, in purple dressed,
Nod o'er the ground-bird's hidden nest.

Thou waitest late, and com'st alone,
When woods are bare and birds are flown,

And frosts and shortening days portend
The aged year is near his end.

Then doth thy sweet and quiet eye
Look through its fringes to the sky,
Blue — blue — as if that sky let fall
A flower from its cerulean wall.

I would that thus, when I shall see
The hour of death draw near to me,
Hope, blossoming within my heart,
May look to heaven as I depart.

EDWARD COATE PINKNEY

21   *A Health*

I FILL this cup to one made up
  Of loveliness alone,
A woman, of her gentle sex
  The seeming paragon;
To whom the better elements
  And kindly stars have given
A form so fair, that, like the air,
  'Tis less of earth than heaven.

Her every tone is music's own,
  Like those of morning birds,
And something more than melody
  Dwells ever in her words;
The coinage of her heart are they,
  And from her lips each flows,

As one may see the burdened bee
    Forth issue from the rose.

Affections are as thoughts to her,
    The measures of her hours;
Her feelings have the fragrancy,
    The freshness of young flowers;
And lovely passions, changing oft,
    So fill her, she appears
The image of themselves by turns, —
    The idol of past years!

Of her bright face one glance will trace
    A picture on the brain,
And of her voice in echoing hearts
    A sound must long remain;
But memory, such as mine of her,
    So very much endears,
When death is nigh my latest sigh
    Will not be life's, but hers.

I fill this cup to one made up
    Of loveliness alone,

A woman, of her gentle sex
    The seeming paragon.
Her health! and would on earth there stood
    Some more of such a frame,
That life might be all poetry,
    And weariness a name.

GEORGE POPE MORRIS

22

Woodman, Spare that Tree

WOODMAN, spare that tree!
  Touch not a single bough!
In youth it sheltered me,
  And I'll protect it now.
'Twas my forefather's hand
  That placed it near his cot;
There, woodman, let it stand,
  Thy axe shall harm it not.

That old familiar tree,
  Whose glory and renown
Are spread o'er land and sea —
  And wouldst thou hew it down?
Woodman, forbear thy stroke!
  Cut not its earth-bound ties;
Oh, spare that aged oak
  Now towering to the skies!

When but an idle boy,
  I sought its grateful shade ;
In all their gushing joy
  Here, too, my sisters played.
My mother kissed me here ;
  My father pressed my hand —
Forgive this foolish tear,
  But let that old oak stand.

My heartstrings round thee cling,
  Close as thy bark, old friend !
Here shall the wild-bird sing,
  And still thy branches bend.
Old tree ! the storm still brave !
  And, woodman, leave the spot ;
While I've a hand to save,
  Thy axe shall harm it not.

ALBERT GORTON GREENE

O'er a low couch the setting sun had thrown its
    latest ray,
Where in his last strong agony a dying warrior
    lay,
The stern old Baron Rudiger, whose frame had
    ne'er been bent
By wasting pain, till time and toil its iron
    strength had spent.

"They come around me here, and say my days
    of life are o'er,
That I shall mount my noble steed and lead my
    band no more;
They come, and to my beard they dare to tell
    me now, that I,
Their own liege lord and master born, — that I,
    ha! ha! must die.

" And what is Death ?   I've dared him oft be-
    fore the Paynim spear, —
Think ye he's entered at my gate, has come to
    seek me here ?
I've met him, faced him, scorned him, when the
    fight was raging hot, —
I'll try his might — I'll brave his power; defy,
    and fear him not.

" Ho ! sound the tocsin from my tower, and fire
    the culverin, —
Bid each retainer arm with speed, — call every
    vassal in,
Up with my banner on the wall, — the banquet
    board prepare ;
Throw wide the portal of my hall, and bring my
    armor there ! "

An hundred hands were busy then — the ban
    quet forth was spread —
And rung the heavy oaken floor with many a
    martial tread,
While from the rich, dark tracery along the
    vaulted wall,

Lights gleamed on harness, plume, and spear,
    o'er the proud old Gothic hall.

Fast hurrying through the outer gate the mailed
    retainers poured,
On through the portal's frowning arch, and
    thronged around the board.
While at its head, within his dark, carved oaken
    chair of state,
Armed cap-à-pie, stern Rudiger, with girded
    falchion, sate.

"Fill every beaker up, my men, pour forth the
    cheering wine;
There's life and strength in every drop, —
    thanksgiving to the vine!
Are ye all there, my vassals true? — mine eyes
    are waxing dim;
Fill round, my tried and fearless ones, each
    goblet to the brim.

"You're there, but yet I see ye not. Draw
    forth each trusty sword

And let me hear your faithful steel clash once
    around my board;
I hear it faintly: — Louder yet! — What clogs
    my heavy breath?
Up all, and shout for Rudiger, 'Defiance unto
    Death!'"

Bowl rang to bowl — steel clanged to steel —
    and rose a deafening cry
That made the torches flare around, and shook
    the flags on high: —
"Ho! cravens, do ye fear him? — Slaves, trai-
    tors! have ye flown?
Ho! cowards, have ye left me to meet him here
    alone!

"But I defy him: — let him come!" Down
    rang the massy cup,
While from its sheath the ready blade came
    flashing halfway up;
And with the black and heavy plumes scarce
    trembling on his head,
There in his dark, carved oaken chair Old
    Rudiger sat, — dead.

SARAH HELEN WHITMAN

24   *A Still Day in Autumn*

1 LOVE to wander through the woodlands hoary
    In the soft light of an autumnal day,
When Summer gathers up her robes of glory,
    And like a dream of beauty glides away.

How through each loved, familiar path she lin-
        gers,
    Serenely smiling through the golden mist,
Tinting the wild grape with her dewy fingers
    Till the cool emerald turns to amethyst;

Kindling the faint stars of the hazel, shining
    To light the gloom of Autumn's mouldering
        halls,
With hoary plumes the clematis entwining
    Where o'er the rock her withered garland
        falls.

Warm lights are on the sleepy uplands waning
  Beneath soft clouds along the horizon rolled,
Till the slant sunbeams through their fringes
   raining
  Bathe all the hills in melancholy gold.

The moist winds breathe of crispèd leaves and
   flowers
  In the damp hollows of the woodland sown,
Mingling the freshness of autumnal showers
  With spicy airs from cedarn alleys blown.

Beside the brook and on the umbered meadow,
  Where yellow fern-tufts fleck the faded
   ground,
With folded lids beneath their palmy shadow
  The gentian nods, in dewy slumbers bound.

Upon those soft, fringed lids the bee sits brood-
   ing,
  Like a fond lover loath to say farewell,
Or with shut wings, through silken folds in-
   truding,
  Creeps near her heart his drowsy tale to tell.

The little birds upon the hillside lonely
  Flit noiselessly along from spray to spray,
Silent as a sweet wandering thought that only
  Shows its bright wings and softly glides
  away.

NATHANIEL PARKER WILLIS

Parrhasius

THERE stood an unsold captive in the mart,
A gray-haired and majestical old man,
Chained to a pillar. It was almost night,
And the last seller from the place had gone,
And not a sound was heard but of a dog
Crunching beneath the stall a refuse bone,
Or the dull echo from the pavement rung,
As the faint captive changed his weary feet.
He had stood there since morning, and had borne
From every eye in Athens the cold gaze
Of curious scorn. The Jew had taunted him
For an Olynthian slave. The buyer came
And roughly struck his palm upon his breast,
And touched his unhealed wounds, and with a
    sneer
Passed on; and when, with weariness o'erspent,
He bowed his head in a forgetful sleep,

The inhuman soldier smote him, and, with threats
Of torture to his children, summoned back
The ebbing blood into his pallid face.

'Twas evening, and the half-descended sun
Tipped with a golden fire the many domes
Of Athens, and a yellow atmosphere
Lay rich and dusky in the shaded street
Through which the captive gazed. He had
    borne up
With a stout heart that long and weary day,
Haughtily patient of his many wrongs,
But now he was alone, and from his nerves
The needless strength departed, and he leaned
Prone on his massy chain, and let his thoughts
Throng on him as they would. Unmarked of
    him
Parrhasius at the nearest pillar stood,
Gazing upon his grief. The Athenian's cheek
Flushed as he measured with a painter's eye
The moving picture. The abandoned limbs,
Stained with the oozing blood, were laced with
    veins

Swollen to purple fulness; the gray hair,
Thin and disordered, hung about his eyes;
And as a thought of wilder bitterness
Rose in his memory, his lips grew white,
And the fast workings of his bloodless face
Told what a tooth of fire was at his heart.

The golden light into the painter's room
Streamed richly, and the hidden colors stole
From the dark pictures radiantly forth,
And in the soft and dewy atmosphere
Like forms and landscapes magical they lay.
The walls were hung with armor, and about
In the dim corners stood the sculptured forms
Of Cytheris, and Dian, and stern Jove,
And from the casement soberly away
Fell the grotesque long shadows, full and true,
And like a veil of filmy mellowness
The lint-specks floated in the twilight air.
Parrhasius stood, gazing forgetfully
Upon his canvas.   There Prometheus lay,
Chained to the cold rocks of Mount Caucasus —
The vulture at his vitals, and the links

Of the lame Lemnian festering in his flesh;
And, as the painter's mind felt through the dim,
Rapt mystery, and plucked the shadows forth
With its far reaching fancy, and with form
And color clad them, his fine, earnest eye
Flashed with a passionate fire, and the quick
    curl
Of his thin nostril, and his quivering lip
Were like the winged god's, breathing from his
    flight.

     " Bring me the captive now !
My hand feels skilful, and the shadows lift
From my waked spirit airily and swift,
    And I could paint the bow
Upon the bended heavens — around me play
Colors of such divinity to-day.

     " Ha ! bind him on his back !
Look ! — as Prometheus in my picture here !
Quick — or he faints ! — stand with the cordial
    near !
    Now — bend him to the rack !

Press down the poisoned links into his flesh !
And tear agape that healing wound afresh !

"So — let him writhe !   How long
Will he live thus ?   Quick, my good pencil,
          now !
What a fine agony works upon his brow !
     Ha ! gray-haired, and so strong !
How fearfully he stifles that short moan !
Gods ! if I could but paint a dying groan !

"'Pity' thee !   So I do !
I pity the dumb victim at the altar —
But does the robed priest for his pity falter ?
     I'd rack thee though I knew
A thousand lives were perishing in thine —
What were ten thousand to a fame like mine !

"'Hereafter !' Ay — hereafter !
A whip to keep a coward to his track !
What gave Death ever from his kingdom back
     To check the sceptic's laughter ?

Come from the grave to-morrow with that
　　story,
And I may take some softer path to glory.

　　"No, no, old man! we die
Even as the flowers, and we shall breathe
　　away
Our life upon the chance wind, even as they!
　　Strain well thy fainting eye —
For when that bloodshot quivering is o'er,
The light of heaven will never reach thee
　　more.

　　"Yet there's a deathless name!
A spirit that the smouldering vault shall
　　spurn,
And like a steadfast planet mount and burn;
　　And though its crown of flame
Consumed my brain to ashes as it shone,
By all the fiery stars! I'd bind it on! —

　　"Ay — though it bid me rifle
My heart's last fount for its insatiate thirst —

Though every life-strung nerve be maddened
    first —
   Though it should bid me stifle
The yearning in my throat for my sweet child,
And taunt its mother till my brain went wild —

    " All — I would do it all —
Sooner than die, like a dull worm, to rot,
Thrust foully into earth to be forgot!
    Oh heavens! — but I appall
Your heart, old man! forgive — ha! on your
    lives
Let him not faint! — rack him till he revives!

    " Vain — vain — give o'er! His eye
Glazes apace. He does not feel you now —
Stand back! I'll paint the death-dew on his
    brow!
    Gods! if he do not die
But for one moment — one — till I eclipse
Conception with the scorn of those calm lips!

    " Shivering! Hark! he mutters
Brokenly now — that was a difficult breath —

Another?   Wilt thou never come, oh Death!
   Look! how his temple flutters!
Is his heart still?   Aha! lift up his head!
He shudders — gasps — Jove help him! —
   so — he's dead."

How like a mounting devil in the heart
Rules the unreined ambition!   Let it once
But play the monarch, and its haughty brow
Glows with a beauty that bewilders thought
And unthrones peace forever.   Putting on
The very pomp of Lucifer, it turns
The heart to ashes, and with not a spring
Left in the bosom for the spirit's lip,
We look upon our splendor and forget
The thirst of which we perish!   Yet hath life
Many a falser idol.   There are hopes
Promising well; and love-touched dreams for
   some;
And passions, many a wild one; and fair schemes
For gold and pleasure — yet will only this
Balk not the soul — Ambition, only, gives,
Even of bitterness, a beaker full!

Friendship is but a slow-awaking dream,
Troubled at best; Love is a lamp unseen,
Burning to waste, or, if its light is found,
Nursed for an idle hour, then idly broken;
Gain is a grovelling care, and Folly tires,
And Quiet is a hunger never fed;
And from Love's very bosom, and from Gain,
Or Folly, or a Friend, or from Repose —
From all but keen Ambition — will the soul
Snatch the first moment of forgetfulness
To wander like a restless child away.
Oh, if there were not better hopes than these —
Were there no palm beyond a feverish fame —
If the proud wealth flung back upon the heart
Must canker in its coffers — if the links
Falsehood hath broken will unite no more —
If the deep yearning love, that hath not found
Its like in the cold world, must waste in tears —
If truth and fervor and devotedness,
Finding no worthy altar, must return
And die of their own fulness — if beyond
The grave there is no heaven in whose wide air
The spirit may find room, and in the love

Of whose bright habitants the lavish heart
May spend itself — what thrice-mocked fools
    are we!

26   *Unseen Spirits*

  THE shadows lay along Broadway,
    'Twas near the twilight-tide,
  And slowly there a lady fair
    Was walking in her pride.
  Alone walked she ; but, viewlessly,
    Walked spirits at her side.

  Peace charmed the street beneath her feet
    And Honor charmed the air ;
  And all astir looked kind on her,
    And called her good as fair,
  For all God ever gave to her
    She kept with chary care.

  She kept with care her beauties rare
    From lovers warm and true,

For her heart was cold to all but gold,
   And the rich came not to woo —
But honored well are charms to sell
   If priests the selling do.

Now walking there was one more fair —
   A slight girl, lily-pale ;
And she had unseen company
   To make the spirit quail :
'Twixt Want and Scorn she walked forlorn,
   And nothing could avail.

No mercy now can clear her brow
   For this world's peace to pray ;
For, as love's wild prayer dissolved in air,
   Her woman's heart gave way ! —
But the sin forgiven by Christ in heaven
   By man is cursed alway !

WILLIAM GILMORE SIMMS

The Lost Pleiad

NOT in the sky,
Where it was seen
So long in eminence of light serene, —
Nor on the white tops of the glistering wave,
Nor down in mansions of the hidden deep,
Though beautiful in green
And crystal, its great caves of mystery, —
Shall the bright watcher have
Her place, and, as of old, high station keep!

Gone! gone!
Oh! nevermore, to cheer
The mariner, who holds his course alone
On the Atlantic, through the weary night,
When the stars turn to watchers, and do sleep,
Shall it again appear,
With the sweet-loving certainty of light,
Down shining on the shut eyes of the deep!

The upward-looking shepherd on the hills
Of Chaldea, night-returning with his flocks,
He wonders why his beauty doth not blaze,
Gladding his gaze, —
And, from his dreary watch along the rocks,
Guiding him homeward o'er the perilous ways!
How stands he waiting still, in a sad maze,
Much wondering, while the drowsy silence fills
The sorrowful vault! — how lingers, in the hope
        that night
May yet renew the expected and sweet light,
So natural to his sight!

And lone,
Where, at the first, in smiling love she shone,
Brood the once happy circle of bright stars:
How should they dream, until her fate was
        known,
That they were ever confiscate to death?
That dark oblivion the pure beauty mars,
And, like the earth, its common bloom and
        breath,
That they should fall from high;

Their lights grow blasted by a touch, and die,
All their concerted springs of harmony
Snapt rudely, and the generous music gone!

Ah! still the strain
Of wailing sweetness fills the saddening sky;
The sister stars, lamenting in their pain
That one of the selectest ones must die, —
Must vanish, when most lovely, from the rest!
Alas! 'tis ever thus the destiny.
Even Rapture's song hath evermore a tone
Of wailing, as for bliss too quickly gone.
The hope most precious is the soonest lost,
The flower most sweet is first to feel the frost.
Are not all short-lived things the loveliest?
And, like the pale star, shooting down the sky
Look they not ever brightest, as they fly
From the lone sphere they blest!

CHARLES FENNO HOFFMAN

It is as she should see herself the while
Nor raid the gazer's fault
Nor Love himself could win her hoe

CHARLES FENNO HOFFMAN

28   *Sparkling and Bright*

SPARKLING and bright in liquid light,
Does the wine our goblets gleam in,
With hue as red as the rosy bed
Which a bee would choose to dream in.
  Then fill to-night, with hearts as light,
    To loves as gay and fleeting
  As bubbles that swim on the beaker's brim,
    And break on the lips while meeting.

Oh! if Mirth might arrest the flight
Of Time through Life's dominions,
We here a while would now beguile
The graybeard of his pinions,
  To drink to-night, with hearts as light,
    To loves as gay and fleeting
  As bubbles that swim on the beaker's brim,
    And break on the lips while meeting.

But since Delight can't tempt the wight,
Nor fond Regret delay him,
Nor Love himself can hold the elf,
Nor sober Friendship stay him,
We'll drink to-night, with hearts as light,
To loves as gay and fleeting
As bubbles that swim on the beaker's brim
And break on the lips while meeting.

EDGAR ALLAN POE

For Annie

THANK Heaven! the crisis —
  The danger — is past,
And the lingering illness
  Is over at last —
And the fever called " Living '
  Is conquered at last.

Sadly, I know
  I am shorn of my strength,
And no muscle I move
  As I lie at full length —
But no matter ! — I feel
  I am better at length.

And I rest so composedly
  Now, in my bed,
That any beholder
  Might fancy me dead —

Might start at beholding me,
   Thinking me dead.

The moaning and groaning,
   The sighing and sobbing,
Are quieted now,
   With that horrible throbbing
At heart : — ah that horrible,
   Horrible throbbing !

The sickness — the nausea —
   The pitiless pain —
Have ceased with the fever
   That maddened my brain —
With the fever called " Living "
   That burned in my brain.

And oh ! of all tortures
   That torture the worst
Has abated — the terrible
   Torture of thirst
For the naphthaline river
   Of Passion accurst : —

I have drank of a water
   That quenches all thirst, —

Of a water that flows,
   With a lullaby sound,
From a spring but a very few
   Feet under ground —
From a cavern not very far
   Down under ground.

And ah! let it never
   Be foolishly said
That my room it is gloomy
   And narrow my bed;
For man never slept
   In a different bed —
And, to *sleep*, you must slumber
   In just such a bed.

My tantalized spirit
   Here blandly reposes,
Forgetting, or never
   Regretting, its roses, —
Its old agitations
   Of myrtles and roses:

For now, while so quietly
   Lying, it fancies
A holier odor
   About it, of pansies —
A rosemary odor,
   Commingled with pansies
With rue and the beautiful
   Puritan pansies.

And so it lies happily,
   Bathing in many
A dream of the truth
   And the beauty of Annie —
Drowned in a bath
   Of the tresses of Annie.

She tenderly kissed me,
   She fondly caressed,
And then I fell gently
   To sleep on her breast —
Deeply to sleep
   From the heaven of her breast.

When the light was extinguished,
   She covered me warm,

And she prayed to the angels
   To keep me from harm —
To the queen of the angels
   To shield me from harm.

And I lie so composedly,
   Now, in my bed,
(Knowing her love)
   That you fancy me dead —
And I rest so contentedly,
   Now, in my bed,
(With her love at my breast)
   That you fancy me dead —
That you shudder to look at me,
   Thinking me dead : —

But my heart it is brighter
   Than all of the many
Stars in the sky,
   For it sparkles with Annie —
It glows with the light
   Of the love of my Annie —
With the thought of the light
   Of the eyes of my Annie.

30   *The Bells*

I

HEAR the sledges with the bells —
        Silver bells!
What a world of merriment their melody fore-
    tells!
        How they tinkle, tinkle, tinkle,
            In the icy air of night!
        While the stars that oversprinkle
        All the heavens, seem to twinkle
            With a crystalline delight;
        Keeping time, time, time,
        In a sort of Runic rhyme,
To the tintinnabulation that so musically wells.
    From the bells, bells, bells, bells,
        Bells, bells, bells —
From the jingling and the tinkling of the bells.

II

Hear the mellow wedding bells —
        Golden bells!

What a world of happiness their harmony fore-
    tells!
      Through the balmy air of night
      How they ring out their delight! —
        From the molten-golden notes,
          And all in tune,
        What a liquid ditty floats
To the turtle-dove that listens, while she gloats
          On the moon!
      Oh, from out the sounding cells,
What a gush of euphony voluminously wells!
        How it swells!
        How it dwells
     On the Future! — How it tells
     Of the rapture that impels
    To the swinging and the ringing
     Of the bells, bells, bells, —
    Of the bells, bells, bells, bells,
      Bells, bells, bells —
To the rhyming and the chiming of the bells!

           III
    Hear the loud alarum bells —
      Brazen bells!

What a tale of terror, now their turbulency
    tells!
        In the startled ear of night
        How they scream out their affright!
        Too much horrified to speak,
        They can only shriek, shriek,
           Out of tune,
In a clamorous appealing to the mercy of the
    fire,
In a mad expostulation with the deaf and frantic
    fire,
        Leaping higher, higher, higher,
        With a desperate desire,
      And a resolute endeavor
      Now — now to sit, or never,
By the side of the pale-faced moon.
        Oh, the bells, bells, bells!
        What a tale their terror tells
          Of Despair!
        How they clang, and clash, and roar!
        What a horror they outpour
On the bosom of the palpitating air!
        Yet the ear it fully knows,

By the twanging,
And the clanging,
How the danger ebbs and flows;
Yet the ear distinctly tells,
In the jangling,
And the wrangling,
How the danger sinks and swells,
By the sinking or the swelling in the anger of
the bells —
Of the bells —
Of the bells, bells, bells, bells,
Bells, bells, bells —
In the clamor and the clanging of the bells!

IV

Hear the tolling of the bells —
Iron bells!
What a world of solemn thought their monody
compels!
In the silence of the night,
How we shiver with affright
At the melancholy menace of their tone!

For every sound that floats
From the rust within their throats
    Is a groan.
And the people — ah, the people —
They that dwell up in the steeple,
    All alone,
And who tolling, tolling, tolling,
  In that muffled monotone,
Feel a glory in so rolling
  On the human heart a stone —
They are neither man nor woman —
They are neither brute nor human —
    They are Ghouls : —
  And their king it is who tolls : —
  And he rolls, rolls, rolls,
    Rolls
  A pæan from the bells !
And his merry bosom swells
  With the pæan of the bells !
And he dances, and he yells ;
  Keeping time, time, time,
  In a sort of Runic rhyme,
To the pæan of the bells : —
    Of the bells :

Keeping time, time, time
In a sort of Runic rhyme,
　　To the throbbing of the bells, —
　Of the bells, bells, bells —
　　To the sobbing of the bells : —
Keeping time, time, time,
　　As he knells, knells, knells,
In a happy Runic rhyme,
　　To the rolling of the bells —
　Of the bells, bells, bells : —
　　To the tolling of the bells —
　Of the bells, bells, bells, bells,
　　Bells, bells, bells —
To the moaning and the groaning of the bells.

31　　　　　*The Raven*

ONCE upon a midnight dreary, while I pondered,
　　weak and weary,
Over many a quaint and curious volume of for-
　　gotten lore —
While I nodded, nearly napping, suddenly there
　　came a tapping,

As of some one gently rapping, rapping at my
   chamber door.
"'Tis some visitor," I muttered, "tapping at
   my chamber door —
                Only this and nothing more."

Ah, distinctly I remember it was in the bleak
   December;
And each separate dying ember wrought its
   ghost upon the floor.
Eagerly I wished the morrow; — vainly I had
   sought to borrow
From my books surcease of sorrow — sorrow
   for the lost Lenore, —
For the rare and radiant maiden whom the
   angels name Lenore —
                Nameless *here* for evermore.

And the silken, sad, uncertain rustling of each
   purple curtain
Thrilled me — filled me with fantastic terrors
   never felt before;
So that now, to still the beating of my heart, I
   stood repeating

"'Tis some visitor entreating entrance at my
    chamber door —
Some late visitor entreating entrance at my
    chamber door ; —
           This it is and nothing more."

Presently my soul grew stronger; hesitating
    then no longer,
"Sir," said I, "or Madam, truly your forgive-
    ness I implore ;
But the fact is I was napping, and so gently you
    came rapping,
And so faintly you came tapping, tapping at my
    chamber door,
That I scarce was sure I heard you." Here I
    opened wide the door ; —
           Darkness there and nothing more.

Deep into that darkness peering, long I stood
    there, wondering, fearing,
Doubting, dreaming dreams no mortal ever
    dared to dream before ;
But the silence was unbroken, and the stillness
    gave no token,

And the only word there spoken was the whispered word, " Lenore ! "
This I whispered, and an echo murmured back
 the word " Lenore ! "
                    Merely this and nothing more.

Back into the chamber turning, all my soul
 within me burning,
Soon again I heard a tapping somewhat louder
 than before.
" Surely," said I, " surely that is something at
 my window-lattice ;
Let me see, then, what thereat is, and this mystery explore —
Let my heart be still a moment and this mystery explore ; —
                    'Tis the wind and nothing more ! "

Open here I flung the shutter, when, with many
 a flirt and flutter
In there stepped a stately Raven of the saintly
 days of yore.
Not the least obeisance made he ; not a minute
 stopped or stayed he ;

But, with mien of lord or lady, perched above
    my chamber door —
Perched upon a bust of Pallas just above my
    chamber door —
        Perched, and sat, and nothing more.

Then this ebony bird beguiling my sad fancy
    into smiling,
By the grave and stern decorum of the counte-
    nance it wore,
"Though thy crest be shorn and shaven, thou,"
    I said, "art sure no craven,
Ghastly grim and ancient Raven wandering
    from the Nightly shore —
Tell me what thy lordly name is on the Night's
    Plutonian shore!"
        Quoth the Raven, "Nevermore."

Much I marvelled this ungainly fowl to hear
    discourse so plainly,
Though its answer little meaning — little rele-
    vancy bore;
For we cannot help agreeing that no living
    human being

Ever yet was blessed with seeing bird above his
    chamber door —
Bird or beast upon the sculptured bust above his
    chamber door,
        With such name as " Nevermore."

But the Raven, sitting lonely on that placid bust,
    spoke only
That one word, as if his soul in that one word
    he did outpour.
Nothing farther then he uttered — not a feather
    then he fluttered —
Till I scarcely more than muttered "Other
    friends have flown before —
On the morrow *he* will leave me, as my hopes
    have flown before."
        Then the bird said " Nevermore."

Startled at the stillness broken by reply so aptly
    spoken,
" Doubtless," said I, "what it utters is its only
    stock and store
Caught from some unhappy master whom un-
    merciful Disaster

Followed fast and followed faster till his songs
    one burden bore —
Till the dirges of his Hope that melancholy bur-
    den bore

            Of ' Never, — nevermore.' "

But the Raven still beguiling all my fancy into
    smiling,
Straight I wheeled a cushioned seat in front of
    bird, and bust and door;
Then, upon the velvet sinking, I betook myself
    to linking
Fancy unto fancy, thinking what this ominous
    bird of yore —
What this grim, ungainly, ghastly, gaunt, and
    ominous bird of yore

            Meant in croaking "Nevermore."

This I sat engaged in guessing, but no syllable
    expressing
To the fowl whose fiery eyes now burned into
    my bosom's core;
This and more I sat divining, with my head at
    ease reclining

On the cushion's velvet lining that the lamp-
  light gloated o'er,
But whose velvet violet lining with the lamp-
  light gloating o'er,
                She shall press, ah, nevermore!

Then, methought, the air grew denser, perfumed
  from an unseen censer
Swung by Seraphim whose foot-falls tinkled on
  the tufted floor.
"Wretch," I cried, "thy God hath lent thee —
  by these angels he hath sent thee
Respite — respite and nepenthe from thy memories of Lenore;
Quaff, oh quaff this kind nepenthe and forget
  this lost Lenore!"
                Quoth the Raven "Nevermore."

"Prophet!" cried I, "thing of evil! prophet
  still, if bird or devil! —
Whether Tempter sent, or whether tempest
  tossed thee here ashore,
Desolate yet all undaunted, on this desert land
  enchanted —

On this home by Horror haunted — tell me truly,
    I implore —
Is there — *is* there balm in Gilead ? — tell me —
    tell me, I implore ! ''
           Quoth the Raven " Nevermore.''

'' Prophet ! '' cried I, " thing of evil ! — prophet
    still, if bird or devil !
By that Heaven that bends above us — by that
    God we both adore —
Tell this soul with sorrow laden if, within the
    distant Aidenn,
It shall clasp a sainted maiden whom the angels
    name Lenore —
Clasp a rare and radiant maiden whom the
    angels name Lenore.''
           Quoth the Raven " Nevermore.''

" Be that word our sign of parting, bird or
    fiend ! '' I shrieked, upstarting —
" Get thee back into the tempest and the Night's
    Plutonian shore !
Leave no black plume as a token of that lie thy
    soul hath spoken !

Leave my loneliness unbroken! — quit the bust
    above my door!
Take thy beak from out my heart, and take thy
    form from off my door!"
           Quoth the Raven "Nevermore."

And the Raven, never flitting, still is sitting,
    still is sitting
On the pallid bust of Pallas just above my
    chamber door;
And his eyes have all the seeming of a demon's
    that is dreaming,
And the lamp-light o'er him streaming throws
    his shadow on the floor;
And my soul from out that shadow that lies
    floating on the floor
           Shall be lifted — *nevermore!*

RALPH WALDO EMERSON

The Humblebee

BURLY dozing humblebee!
Where thou art is clime for me.
Let them sail for Porto Rique,
Far-off heats through seas to seek,
I will follow thee alone,
Thou animated torrid zone!
Zig-zag steerer, desert cheerer,
Let me chase thy waving lines;
Keep me nearer, me thy hearer,
Singing over shrubs and vines.

Insect lover of the sun,
Joy of thy dominion!
Sailor of the atmosphere,
Swimmer through the waves of air,
Voyager of light and noon,
Epicurean of June,
Wait I prithee, till I come

Within ear-shot of thy hum, —
All without is martyrdom.

When the south wind, in May days,
With a net of shining haze,
Silvers the horizon wall,
And, with softness touching all,
Tints the human countenance
With a color of romance,
And, infusing subtle heats,
Turns the sod to violets,
Thou in sunny solitudes,
Rover of the underwoods,
The green silence dost displace,
With thy mellow breezy bass.

Hot midsummer's petted crone,
Sweet to me thy drowsy tone,
Telling of countless sunny hours,
Long days, and solid banks of flowers,
Of gulfs of sweetness without bound
In Indian wildernesses found,
Of Syrian peace, immortal leisure,
Firmest cheer and bird-like pleasure.

Aught unsavory or unclean,
Hath my insect never seen,
But violets and bilberry bells,
Maple sap and daffodels,
Grass with green flag half-mast high,
Succory to match the sky,
Columbine with horn of honey,
Scented fern, and agrimony,
Clover, catchfly, adders-tongue,
And brier-roses dwelt among;
All beside was unknown waste,
All was picture as he passed.

Wiser far than human seer,
Yellow-breeched philosopher!
Seeing only what is fair,
Sipping only what is sweet,
Thou dost mock at fate and care,
Leave the chaff and take the wheat.
When the fierce north-western blast
Cools sea and land so far and fast,
Thou already slumberest deep, —
Woe and want thou canst out-sleep, —

Want and woe which torture us,
Thy sleep makes ridiculous.

33   *The Rhodora*

LINES ON BEING ASKED, WHENCE IS THE FLOWER

IN May, when sea-winds pierced our solitudes,
I found the fresh Rhodora in the woods,
Spreading its leafless blooms in a damp nook,
To please the desert and the sluggish brook:
The purple petals fallen in the pool
Made the black water with their beauty gay,
Here might the redbird come his plumes to
    cool,
And court the flower that cheapens his array.
Rhodora! if the sages ask thee why
This charm is wasted on the earth and sky,
Dear, tell them, that if eyes were made for
    seeing,
Then beauty is its own excuse for being.
Why thou wert there, O rival of the rose!
I never thought to ask, I never knew,

But in my simple ignorance suppose
The selfsame Power that brought me there
    brought you.

34   *Each and All*

LITTLE thinks, in the field, yon red-cloaked
    clown,
Of thee, from the hill-top looking down;
And the heifer, that lows in the upland farm,
Far-heard, lows not thine ear to charm;
The sexton tolling the bell at noon,
Dreams not that great Napoleon
Stops his horse, and lists with delight,
Whilst his files sweep round yon Alpine height;
Nor knowest thou what argument
Thy life to thy neighbor's creed has lent:
All are needed by each one,
Nothing is fair or good alone.

I thought the sparrow's note from heaven,
Singing at dawn on the alder bough;
I brought him home in his nest at even; —
He sings the song, but it pleases not now,

For I did not bring home the river and sky;
He sang to my ear; they sang to my eye.
The delicate shells lay on the shore;
The bubbles of the latest wave
Fresh pearls to their enamel gave;
And the bellowing of the savage sea
Greeted their safe escape to me;
I wiped away the weeds and foam,
And fetched my sea-born treasures home;
But the poor, unsightly, noisome things
Had left their beauty on the shore
With the sun, and the sand, and the wild
    uproar.

The lover watched his graceful maid
As 'mid the virgin train she strayed,
Nor knew her beauty's best attire
Was woven still by the snow-white quire,
At last she came to his hermitage,
Like the bird from the woodlands to the cage, —
The gay enchantment was undone,
A gentle wife, but fairy none.
    Then I said, "I covet Truth;

Beauty is unripe childhood's cheat, —
I leave it behind with the games of youth."
As I spoke, beneath my feet
The ground-pine curled its pretty wreath,
Running over the club-moss burrs;
I inhaled the violet's breath;
Around me stood the oaks and firs;
Pine cones and acorns lay on the ground;
Above me soared the eternal sky,
Full of light and deity;
Again I saw, again I heard,
The rolling river, the morning bird; —
Beauty through my senses stole,
I yielded myself to the perfect whole.

35   *The Problem*

I LIKE a church, I like a cowl,
I love a prophet of the soul,
And on my heart monastic aisles
Fall like sweet strains or pensive smiles;
Yet not for all his faith can see,
Would I that cowlèd churchman be.

Why should the vest on him allure,
Which I could not on me endure?

Not from a vain or shallow thought
His awful Jove young Phidias brought;
Never from lips of cunning fell
The thrilling Delphic oracle;
Out from the heart of nature rolled
The burdens of the Bible old;
The litanies of nations came,
Like the volcano's tongue of flame,
Up from the burning core below,
The canticles of love and woe.
The hand that rounded Peter's dome,
And groined the aisles of Christian Rome,
Wrought in a sad sincerity,
Himself from God he could not free;
He builded better than he knew,
The conscious stone to beauty grew.

Know'st thou what wove yon woodbird's nest
Of leaves and feathers from her breast;
Or how the fish outbuilt its shell,
Painting with morn each annual cell;

Or how the sacred pine tree adds
To her old leaves new myriads?
Such and so grew these holy piles,
Whilst love and terror laid the tiles.
Earth proudly wears the Parthenon
As the best gem upon her zone;
And Morning opes with haste her lids
To gaze upon the Pyramids;
O'er England's abbeys bends the sky
As on its friends with kindred eye;
For out of Thought's interior sphere
These wonders rose to upper air,
And nature gladly gave them place,
Adopted them into her race,
And granted them an equal date
With Andes and with Ararat.

These temples grew as grows the grass,
Art might obey but not surpass.
The passive Master lent his hand
To the vast soul that o'er him planned,
And the same power that reared the shrine
Bestrode the tribes that knelt within.

Even the fiery Pentecost
Girds with one flame the countless host,
Trances the heart through chanting quires,
And through the priest the mind inspires.

The word unto the prophet spoken
Was writ on tables yet unbroken;
The word by seers or sibyls told
In groves of oak, or fanes of gold,
Still floats upon the morning wind,
Still whispers to the willing mind.
One accent of the Holy Ghost
The heedless world hath never lost.
I know what say the Fathers wise,
The Book itself before me lies,
Old *Chrysostom*, best Augustine,
And he who blent both in his line,
The younger *Golden-lips* or mines,
Taylor, the Shakespeare of divines,
His words are music in my ear,
I see his cowlèd portrait dear,
And yet for all his faith could see,
I would not the good bishop be.

36   *Good-by*

GOOD-BY, proud world, I'm going home,
Thou'rt not my friend, and I'm not thine;
Long through thy weary crowds I roam;
A river ark on the ocean brine,
Long I've been tossed like the driven foam
But now, proud world, I'm going home.

Good-by to Flattery's fawning face,
To Grandeur, with his wise grimace,
To upstart Wealth's averted eye,
To supple Office low and high,
To crowded halls, to court, and street,
To frozen hearts, and hasting feet,
To those who go, and those who come,
Good-by, proud world, I'm going home.

I'm going to my own hearth-stone
Bosomed in yon green hills, alone,
A secret nook in a pleasant land,
Whose groves the frolic fairies planned;
Where arches green the livelong day
Echo the blackbird's roundelay,

And vulgar feet have never trod
A spot that is sacred to thought and **God**.

Oh, when I am safe in my sylvan home,
I tread on the pride of Greece and Rome;
And when I am stretched beneath the pines
Where the evening star so holy shines,
I laugh at the lore and the pride of man,
At the sophist schools, and the learned clan;
For what are they all in their high conceit,
When man in the bush with God may meet.

ISAAC McLELLAN

37   *New England's Dead*

NEW ENGLAND's dead !   New England's dead
    On every hill they lie ;
On every field of strife, made red
    By bloody victory.
Each valley, where the battle poured
    Its red and awful tide,
Beheld the brave New England sword
    With slaughter deeply dyed.
Their bones are on the northern hill,
    And on the southern plain,
By brook and river, lake and rill,
    And by the roaring main.

The land is holy where they fought,
    And holy where they fell ;
For by their blood that land was bought,
    The land they loved so well.

Then glory to that valiant band,
The honored saviors of the land!

Oh, few and weak their numbers were, –
    A handful of brave men;
But to their God they gave their prayer,
    And rushed to battle then.
The God of battles heard their cry,
And sent to them the victory.

They left the ploughshare in the mould,
Their flocks and herds without a fold,
The sickle in the unshorn grain,
The corn, half-garnered, on the plain,
And mustered, in their simple dress,
For wrongs to seek a stern redress,
To right those wrongs, come weal, come woe,
To perish, or o'ercome their foe.

And where are ye, O fearless men?
    And where are ye to-day?
I call : — the hills reply again
    That ye have passed away;

That on old Bunker's lonely height,
    In Trenton, and in Monmouth ground,
The grass grows green, the harvest bright
    Above each soldier's mound.
The bugle's wild and warlike blast
    Shall muster them no more;
An army now might thunder past,
    And they heed not its roar.
The starry flag, 'neath which they fought
    In many a bloody day,
From their old graves shall rouse them not,
    For they have passed away.

HENRY WADSWORTH LONGFELLOW

38   *Hymn to the Night*

Ἀσπασίη, τρίλλιστος

Πότνια, πότνια νύξ,
ὑπνοδότειρα τῶν πολυπόνων βροτῶν,
Ἐρεβόθεν ἴθι· μόλε μόλε κατάπτερος
Ἀγαμεμνόνιον ἐπὶ δόμον·
ὑπὸ γὰρ ἀλγέων, ὑπό τε συμφορᾶς
διοιχόμεθ', οἰχόμεθα.

EURIPIDES.

I HEARD the trailing garments of the Night
    Sweep through her marble halls!
I saw her sable skirts all fringed with light
    From the celestial walls!

I felt her presence, by its spell of might,
    Stoop o'er me from above;
The calm, majestic presence of the Night,
    As of the one I love.

I heard the sounds of sorrow and delight,
    The manifold, soft chimes,

That fill the haunted chambers of the Night,
    Like some old poet's rhymes.

From the cool cisterns of the midnight air
    My spirit drank repose;
The fountain of perpetual peace flows there, —
    From those deep cisterns flows.

O holy Night! from thee I learn to bear
    What man has borne before!
Thou layest thy finger on the lips of Care,
    And they complain no more.

Peace! Peace! Orestes-like I breathe this
    prayer!
    Descend with broad-winged flight,
The welcome, the thrice-prayed for, the most
    fair,
    The best-belovèd Night!

39   *The Arsenal at Springfield*

THIS is the Arsenal. From floor to ceiling,
    Like a huge organ, rise the burnished arms;

But from their silent pipes no anthem pealing
　　Startles the villages with strange alarms.

Ah! what a sound will rise, how wild and
　　　dreary,
　　When the death-angel touches those swift
　　　keys!
What loud lament and dismal Miserere
　　Will mingle with their awful symphonies!

I hear even now the infinite fierce chorus,
　　The cries of agony, the endless groan,
Which, through the ages that have gone before
　　us,
　　In long reverberations reach our own.

On helm and harness rings the Saxon hammer,
　　Through Cimbric forest roars the Norseman's
　　　song,
And loud, amid the universal clamor,
　　O'er distant deserts sounds the Tartar gong.

I hear the Florentine, who from his palace
　　Wheels out his battle-bell with dreadful din,

And Aztec priests upon their teocallis
    Beat the wild war-drums made of serpent's
      skin;

The tumult of each sacked and burning village;
    The shout that every prayer for mercy
      drowns;
The soldiers' revels in the midst of pillage;
    The wail of famine in beleaguered towns;

The bursting shell, the gateway wrenched asun·
      der,
    The rattling musketry, the clashing blade;
And ever and anon, in tones of thunder,
    The diapason of the cannonade.

Is it, O man, with such discordant noises,
    With such accursed instruments as these,
Thou drownest Nature's sweet and kindly
      voices,
    And jarrest the celestial harmonies?

Were half the power, that fills the world with
      terror,

Were half the wealth, bestowed on camps
and courts,
Given to redeem the human mind from error,
There were no need of arsenals nor forts :

The warrior's name would be a name abhorred !
And every nation that should lift again
Its hand against a brother, on its forehead
Would wear for evermore the curse of Cain !

Down the dark future, through long genera-
tions.
The echoing sounds grow fainter and then
cease ;
And like a bell, with solemn, sweet vibrations,
I hear once more the voice of Christ say,
" Peace ! "

Peace ! and no longer from its brazen portals
The blast of War's great organ shakes the
skies !
But beautiful as songs of the immortals,
The holy melodies of love arise.

40   *The Fire of Driftwood*

WE sat within the farm-house old,
    Whose windows, looking o'er the bay,
Gave to the sea-breeze, damp and cold,
    An easy entrance, night and day.

Not far away we saw the port, —
    The strange, old-fashioned, silent town,
The lighthouse, — the dismantled fort, —
    The wooden houses, quaint and brown.

We sat and talked until the night,
    Descending, filled the little room;
Our faces faded from the sight
    Our voices only broke the gloom.

We spake of many a vanished scene,
    Of what we once had thought and said,
Of what had been, and might have been,
    And who was changed, and who was dead;

And all that fills the hearts of friends,
    When first they feel, with secret pain,

Their lives thenceforth have separate ends,
    And never can be one again;

The first slight swerving of the heart,
    That words are powerless to express,
And leave it still unsaid in part,
    Or say it in too great excess.

The very tones in which we spake
    Had something strange, I could but mark;
The leaves of memory seemed to make
    A mournful rustling in the dark.

Oft died the words upon our lips,
    As suddenly, from out the fire
Built of the wreck of stranded ships,
    The flames would leap and then expire.

And, as their splendor flashed and failed,
    We thought of wrecks upon the main,
Of ships dismasted, that were hailed
    And sent no answer back again.

The windows, rattling in their frames, —
    The ocean, roaring up the beach, —

The gusty blast, — the bickering flames, —
   All mingled vaguely in our speech;

Until they made themselves a part
   Of fancies floating through the brain, —
The long-lost ventures of the heart,
   That send no answers back again.

O flames that glowed! O hearts that yearned!
   They were indeed too much akin,
The driftwood fire without that burned,
   The thoughts that burned and glowed within.

41   *Resignation*

THERE is no flock, however watched and tended,
   But one dead lamb is there!
There is no fireside, howsoe'er defended,
   But has one vacant chair!

The air is full of farewells to the dying,
   And mournings for the dead;
The heart of Rachel, for her children crying,
   Will not be comforted!

Let us be patient! These severe afflictions
   Not from the ground arise,
But oftentimes celestial benedictions
   Assume this dark disguise.

We see but dimly through the mists and vapors;
   Amid these earthly damps
What seem to us but sad, funereal tapers
   May be heaven's distant lamps.

There is no Death! What seems so is transi-
   tion.
   This life of mortal breath
Is but a suburb of the life elysian,
   Whose portal we call Death.

She is not dead, — the child of our affection, —
   But gone unto that school
Where she no longer needs our poor protection,
   And Christ himself doth rule.

In that great cloister's stillness and seclusion,
   By guardian angels led,
Safe from temptation, safe from sin's pollution,
   She lives, whom we call dead.

Day after day we think what she is doing
    In those bright realms of air;
Year after year, her tender steps pursuing,
    Behold her grown more fair.

Thus do we walk with her, and keep unbroken
    The bond which nature gives,
Thinking that our remembrance, though un
        spoken,
    May reach her where she lives.

Not as a child shall we again behold her;
    For when with raptures wild
In our embraces we again enfold her,
    She will not be a child;

But a fair maiden, in her Father's mansion,
    Clothed with celestial grace;
And beautiful with all the soul's expansion
    Shall we behold her face.

And though at times impetuous with emotion
    And anguish long suppressed,

The swelling heart heaves moaning like the
    ocean,
  That cannot be at rest, —

We will be patient, and assuage the feeling
  We may not wholly stay;
By silence sanctifying, not concealing,
  The grief that must have way.

42   *Sea-weed*

  WHEN descends on the Atlantic
      The gigantic
  Storm-wind of the equinox,
  Landward in his wrath he scourges
      The toiling surges,
  Laden with sea-weed from the rocks:

  From Bermuda's reefs; from edges
      Of sunken ledges,
  In some far-off, bright Azore;
  From Bahama, and the dashing,
      Silver-flashing
  Surges of San Salvador;

From the tumbling surf, that buries
    The Orkneyan skerries,
Answering the hoarse Hebrides;
And from wrecks of ships, and drifting
    Spars, uplifting
On the desolate, rainy seas; —

Ever drifting, drifting, drifting
    On the shifting
Currents of the restless main;
Till in sheltered coves, and reaches
    Of sandy beaches,
All have found repose again.

So when storms of wild emotion
    Strike the ocean
Of the poet's soul, erelong,
From each cave and rocky fastness
    In its vastness,
Floats some fragment of a song:

From the far-off isles enchanted
    Heaven has planted
With the golden fruit of Truth;

From the flashing surf, whose vision
    Gleams Elysian
In the tropic clime of Youth;

From the strong Will, and the Endeavor
    That forever
Wrestles with the tides of Fate;
From the wreck of Hopes far-scattered,
    Tempest-shattered,
Floating waste and desolate; —

Ever drifting, drifting, drifting
    On the shifting
Currents of the restless heart;
Till at length in books recorded,
    They, like hoarded
Household words, no more depart.

43   *The Day is Done*

THE day is done, and the darkness
    Falls from the wings of Night,
As a feather is wafted downward
    From an eagle in his flight.

I see the lights of the village
  Gleam through the rain and the mist,
And a feeling of sadness comes o'er me,
  That my soul cannot resist:

A feeling of sadness and longing,
  That is not akin to pain,
And resembles sorrow only
  As the mist resembles the rain.

Come, read to me some poem,
  Some simple and heartfelt lay,
That shall soothe this restless feeling,
  And banish the thoughts of day.

Not from the grand old masters,
  Not from the bards sublime,
Whose distant footsteps echo
  Through the corridors of Time.

For like strains of martial music,
  Their mighty thoughts suggest
Life's endless toil and endeavor;
  And to-night I long for rest.

Read from some humbler poet,
  Whose songs gushed from his heart,
As showers from the clouds of summer,
  Or tears from the eyelids start;

Who, through long days of labor,
  And nights devoid of ease,
Still heard in his soul the music
  Of wonderful melodies.

Such songs have power to quiet
  The restless pulse of care,
And come like the benediction
  That follows after prayer.

Then read from the treasured volume
  The poem of thy choice,
And lend to the rhyme of the poet
  The beauty of thy voice.

And the night shall be filled with music,
  And the cares that infest the day,
Shall fold their tents, like the Arabs,
  And as silently steal away.

JOHN GREENLEAF WHITTIER

The Angel of Patience

A FREE PARAPHRASE OF THE GERMAN

To weary hearts, to mourning homes,
God's meekest Angel gently comes:
No power has he to banish pain,
Or give us back our lost again;
And yet in tenderest love our dear
And heavenly Father sends him here.

There's quiet in that Angel's glance,
There's rest in his still countenance!
He mocks no grief with idle cheer,
Nor wounds with words the mourner's ear
But ills and woes he may not cure
He kindly trains us to endure.

Angel of Patience! sent to calm
Our feverish brows with cooling palm;
To lay the storms of hope and fear,
And reconcile life's smile and tear;

The throbs of wounded pride to still,
And make our own our Father's will!

O thou who mournest on thy way,
With longings for the close of day;
He walks with thee, that Angel kind,
And gently whispers, "Be resigned:
Bear up, bear on, the end shall tell
The dear Lord ordereth all things well!"

45   *The Barefoot Boy*

BLESSINGS on thee, little man,
Barefoot boy, with cheek of tan!
With thy turned-up pantaloons,
And thy merry whistled tunes;
With thy red lip, redder still
Kissed by strawberries on the hill;
With the sunshine on thy face,
Through thy torn brim's jaunty grace;
From my heart I give thee joy, —
I was once a barefoot boy!
Prince thou art, — the grown-up man
Only is republican.

Let the million-dollared ride!
Barefoot, trudging at his side,
Thou hast more than he can buy
In the reach of ear and eye, —
Outward sunshine, inward joy:
Blessings on thee, barefoot boy!

O for boyhood's painless play,
Sleep that wakes in laughing day,
Health that mocks the doctor's rules,
Knowledge never learned of schools,
Of the wild bee's morning chase,
Of the wild-flower's time and place,
Flight of fowl and habitude
Of the tenants of the wood;
How the tortoise bears his shell,
How the woodchuck digs his cell,
And the ground-mole sinks his well;
How the robin feeds her young,
How the oriole's nest is hung;
Where the whitest lilies blow,
Where the freshest berries grow,
Where the groundnut trails its vine,

Where the wood-grape's clusters shine
Of the black wasp's cunning way,
Mason of his walls of clay,
And the architectural plans
Of gray hornet artisans! —
For, eschewing books and tasks,
Nature answers all he asks;
Hand in hand with her he walks,
Face to face with her he talks,
Part and parcel of her joy, —
Blessings on the barefoot boy!

O for boyhood's time of June.
Crowding years in one brief moon,
When all things I heard or saw,
Me, their master, waited for.
I was rich in flowers and trees,
Humming-birds and honey-bees;
For my sport the squirrel played,
Plied the snouted mole his spade;
For my taste the blackberry cone
Purpled over hedge and stone;
Laughed the brook for my delight

Through the day and through the night,
Whispering at the garden wall,
Talked with me from fall to fall;
Mine the sand-rimmed pickerel pond,
Mine the walnut slopes beyond,
Mine, on bending orchard trees,
Apples of Hesperides!
Still as my horizon grew,
Larger grew my riches too;
All the world I saw or knew
Seemed a complex Chinese toy,
Fashioned for a barefoot boy!

O for festal dainties spread,
Like my bowl of milk and bread, —
Pewter spoon and bowl of wood,
On the door-stone, gray and rude!
O'er me, like a regal tent,
Cloudy-ribbed, the sunset bent,
Purple-curtained, fringed with gold,
Looped in many a wind-swung fold;
While for music came the play
Of the pied frogs' orchestra:

And, to light the noisy choir,
Lit the fly his lamp of fire.
I was monarch : pomp and joy
Waited on the barefoot boy !

Cheerily, then, my little man,
Live and laugh, as boyhood can !
Though the flinty slopes be hard,
Stubble-speared the new-mown sward
Every morn shall lead thee through
Fresh baptisms of the dew ;
Every evening from thy feet
Shall the cool wind kiss the heat :
All too soon these feet must hide
In the prison cells of pride,
Lose the freedom of the sod,
Like a colt's for work be shod,
Made to tread the mills of toil,
Up and down in ceaseless moil :
Happy if their track be found
Never on forbidden ground ;
Happy if they sink not in
Quick and treacherous sands of sin.

Ah! that thou couldst know thy joy,
  Ere it passes, barefoot boy!

46   *Burns*

ON RECEIVING A SPRIG OF HEATHER IN BLOSSOM

No more these simple flowers belong
  To Scottish maid and lover,
Sown in the common soil of song,
  They bloom the wide world over.

In smiles and tears, in sun and showers,
  The minstrel and the heather,
The deathless singer and the flowers
  He sang of live together.

Wild heather-bells and Robert Burns!
  The moorland flower and peasant!
How, at their mention, memory turns
  Her pages old and pleasant!

The gray sky wears again its gold
  And purple of adorning,
And manhood's noonday shadows hold
  The dews of boyhood's morning:

The dews that washed the dust and soil
　　From off the wings of pleasure,
The sky, that flecked the ground of toil
　　With golden threads of leisure.

I call to mind the summer day,
　　The early harvest mowing,
The sky with sun and clouds at play,
　　And flowers with breezes blowing.

I hear the blackbird in the corn,
　　The locust in the haying;
And, like the fabled hunter's horn,
　　Old tunes my heart is playing.

How oft that day, with fond delay,
　　I sought the maple's shadow,
And sang with Burns the hours away,
　　Forgetful of the meadow!

Bees hummed, birds twittered, overhead
　　I heard the squirrels leaping,
The good dog listened while I read,
　　And wagged his tail in keeping.

I watched him while in sportive mood
  I read " The Twa Dogs' " story,
And half believed he understood
  The poet's allegory.

Sweet day, sweet songs!—The golden hours
  Grew brighter for that singing,
From brook and bird and meadow flowers
  A dearer welcome bringing.

New light on home-seen Nature beamed,
  New glory over Woman;
And daily life and duty seemed
  No longer poor and common.

I woke to find the simple truth
  Of fact and feeling better
Than all the dreams that held my youth
  A still repining debtor:

That Nature gives her handmaid, Art,
  The themes of sweet discoursing;
The tender idyls of the heart
  In every tongue rehearsing.

Why dream of lands of gold and pearl,
  Of loving knight and lady,
When farmer boy and barefoot girl
  Were wandering there already?

I saw through all familiar things
  The romance underlying;
The joys and griefs that plume the wings
  Of Fancy skyward flying.

I saw the same blithe day return,
  The same sweet fall of even,
That rose on wooded Craigie-burn,
  And sank on crystal Devon.

I matched with Scotland's heathery hills
  The sweet-brier and the clover;
With Ayr and Doon, my native rills,
  Their wood-hymns chanting over.

O'er rank and pomp, as he had seen,
  I saw the Man uprising;
No longer common or unclean,
  The child of God's baptizing!

With clearer eyes I saw the worth
   Of life among the lowly;
The Bible at his Cotter's hearth
   Had made my own more holy.

And if at times an evil strain,
   To lawless love appealing,
Broke in upon the sweet refrain
   Of pure and healthful feeling,

It died upon the eye and ear,
   No inward answer gaining;
No heart had I to see or hear
   The discord and the staining.

Let those who never erred forget
   His worth, in vain bewailings;
Sweet Soul of Song! — I own my debt
   Uncancelled by his failings!

Lament who will the ribald line
   Which tells his lapse from duty,
How kissed the maddening lips of wine
   Or wanton ones of beauty;

But think, while falls that shade between
    The erring one and Heaven,
That he who loved like Magdalen,
    Like her may be forgiven.

Not his the song whose thunderous chime
    Eternal echoes render, —
The mournful Tuscan's haunted rhyme,
    And Milton's starry splendor!

But who his human heart has laid
    To Nature's bosom nearer?
Who sweetened toil like him, or paid
    To love a tribute dearer?

Through all his tuneful art, how strong
    The human feeling gushes!
The very moonlight of his song
    Is warm with smiles and blushes!

Give lettered pomp to teeth of Time,
    So "Bonnie Doon" but tarry;
Blot out the Epic's stately rhyme,
    But spare his "Highland Mary"!

47   *The Reformer*

ALL grim and soiled and brown with tan,
   I saw a Strong One, in his wrath,
Smiting the godless shrines of man
         Along his path.

The Church, beneath her trembling dome
   Essayed in vain her ghostly charm:
Wealth shook within his gilded home
         With strange alarm.

Fraud from his secret chambers fled
   Before the sunlight bursting in:
Sloth drew her pillow o'er her head
         To drown the din.

"Spare," Art implored, "yon holy pile;
   That grand, old, time-worn turret spare;
Meek Reverence, kneeling in the aisle,
         Cried out, "Forbear!"

Gray-bearded Use, who, deaf and blind,
   Groped for his old accustomed stone,

Leaned on his staff, and wept to find
    His seat o'erthrown.

Young Romance raised his dreamy eyes,
    O'erhung with paly locks of gold, —
"Why smite," he asked in sad surprise,
    "The fair, the old?"

Yet louder rang the Strong One's stroke
    Yet nearer flashed his axe's gleam;
Shuddering and sick of heart I woke,
    As from a dream.

I looked: aside the dust-cloud rolled, —
    The Waster seemed the Builder too;
Up springing from the ruined Old
    I saw the New.

'Twas but the ruin of the bad, —
    The wasting of the wrong and ill;
Whate'er of good the old time had
    Was living still.

Calm grew the brows of him I feared;
    The frown which awed me passed away,

And left behind a smile which cheered
    Like breaking day.

The grain grew green on battle-plains,
  O'er swarded war-mounds grazed the cow;
The slave stood forging from his chains
    The spade and plough.

Where frowned the fort, pavilions gay
  And cottage windows, flower-entwined,
Looked out upon the peaceful bay
    And hills behind.

Through vine-wreathed cups with wine once
    red,
  The lights on brimming crystal fell,
Drawn, sparkling, from the rivulet head
    And mossy well.

Through prison-walls, like Heaven-sent hope,
  Fresh breezes blew, and sunbeams strayed,
And with the idle gallows-rope
    The young child played.

Where the doomed victim in his cell
  Had counted o'er the weary hours,

Glad school-girls, answering to the bell,
  Came crowned with flowers.

Grown wiser for the lesson given,
  I fear no longer, for I know
That, where the share is deepest driven,
  The best fruits grow.

The outworn rite, the old abuse,
  The pious fraud transparent grown,
The good held captive in the use
  Of wrong alone, —

These wait their doom, from that great law
  Which makes the past time serve to-day:
And fresher life the world shall draw
  From their decay.

O, backward-looking son of time!
  The new is old, the old is new,
The cycle of a change sublime
  Still sweeping through.

So wisely taught the Indian seer;
  Destroying Seva, forming Brahm,

Who wake by turns Earth's love and fear,
    Are one, the same.

As idly as, in that old day,
    Thou mournest, did thy sires repine,
So, in his time, thy child grown gray
    Shall sigh for thine.

Yet, not the less for them or thou
    The eternal step of Progress beats
To that great anthem, calm and slow,
    Which God repeats!

Take heart! — the Waster builds again,
    A charmèd life old Goodness hath;
The tares may perish, — but the grain
    Is not for death.

God works in all things; all obey
    His first propulsion from the night:
Ho, wake and watch! — the world is gray
    With morning light!

48   *The Eve of Election*

FROM gold to gray
Our mild sweet day
Of Indian summer fades too soon;
But tenderly
Above the sea
Hangs, white and calm, the hunter's moon.

In its pale fire,
The village spire
Shows like the zodiac's spectral lance;
The painted walls
Whereon it falls
Transfigured stand in marble trance!

O'er fallen leaves
The west-wind grieves,
Yet comes a seed-time round again;
And morn shall see
The State sown free
With baleful tares or healthful grain.

Along the street
The shadows meet
Of Destiny, whose hands conceal
The moulds of fate
That shape the State,
And make or mar the common weal.

Around I see
The powers that be;
I stand by Empire's primal springs;
And princes meet
In every street,
And hear the tread of uncrowned kings!

Hark! through the crowd
The laugh runs loud,
Beneath the sad, rebuking moon.
God save the land,
A careless hand
May shake or swerve ere morrow's noon!

No jest is this;
One cast amiss
May blast the hope of Freedom's year.

O, take me where
Are hearts of prayer,
And foreheads bowed in reverent fear!

Not lightly fall
Beyond recall
The written scrolls a breath can float;
The crowning fact,
The kingliest act
Of Freedom is the freeman's vote!

For pearls that gem
A diadem
The diver in the deep sea dies;
The regal right
We boast to-night
Is ours through costlier sacrifice;

The blood of Vane,
His prison pain
Who traced the path the pilgrim trod,
And hers whose faith
Drew strength from death,
And prayed her Russell up to God!

Our hearts grow cold,
We lightly hold
A right which brave men died to gain;
The stake, the cord,
The axe, the sword,
Grim nurses at its birth of pain.

The shadow rend,
And o'er us bend,
O martyrs, with your crowns and palms, —
Breathe through these throngs
Your battle songs,
Your scaffold prayers and dungeon psalms!

Look from the sky,
Like God's great eye,
Thou solemn moon, with searching beam;
Till in the sight
Of thy pure light
Our mean self-seekings meaner seem.

Shame from our hearts
Unworthy arts,
The fraud designed, the purpose dark;

And smite away
The hands we lay
Profanely on the sacred ark.

To party claims
And private aims,
Reveal that august face of Truth,
Whereto are given
The age of heaven,
The beauty of immortal youth.

So shall our voice
Of sovereign choice
Swell the deep bass of duty done,
And strike the key
Of time to be,
When God and man shall speak as one!

OLIVER WENDELL HOLMES

49 *The Chambered Nautilus*

THIS is the ship of pearl, which, poets feign,
　　Sails the unshadowed main, —
　　The venturous bark that flings
On the sweet summer wind its purpled wings
In gulfs enchanted, where the siren sings,
　　And coral reefs lie bare,
Where the cold sea-maids rise to sun their
　　streaming hair.

Its webs of living gauze no more unfurl;
　　Wrecked is the ship of pearl!
　　And every chambered cell,
Where its dim dreaming life was wont to dwell,
As the frail tenant shaped his growing shell,
　　Before thee lies revealed, —
Its irised ceiling rent, its sunless crypt unsealed!

Year after year beheld the silent toil
    That spread his lustrous coil;
    Still, as the spiral grew,
He left the past year's dwelling for the new,
Stole with soft step its shining archway through,
    Built up its idle door,
Stretched in his last-found home, and knew the
    old no more.

Thanks for the heavenly message brought by
    thee,
    Child of the wandering sea,
    Cast from her lap forlorn!
From thy dead lips a clearer note is born
Than ever Triton blew from wreathèd horn!
    While on mine ear it rings,
Through the deep caves of thought I hear a
    voice that sings:—

Build thee more stately mansions, O my soul,
    As the swift seasons roll!
    Leave thy low-vaulted past!

Let each new temple, nobler than the last,
Shut thee from heaven with a dome more vast,
    Till thou at length art free,
Leaving thine outgrown shell by life's unresting
      sea!

50   *Old Ironsides* [1]

    Ay, tear her tattered ensign down!
        Long has it waved on high,
    And many an eye has danced to see
        That banner in the sky;
    Beneath it rung the battle shout,
        And burst the cannon's roar; —
    The meteor of the ocean air
        Shall sweep the clouds no more.

    Her deck, once red with heroes' blood,
        Where knelt the vanquished foe,
    When winds were hurrying o'er the flood,
        And waves were white below,

[1] Verses, the popularity of which averted the proposed breaking up of the old frigate *Constitution*, then lying at the Navy Yard in Charlestown, Mass.

No more shall feel the victor's tread,
    Or know the conquered knee; —
The harpies of the shore shall pluck
    The eagle of the sea!

Oh, better that her shattered hulk
    Should sink beneath the wave;
Her thunders shook the mighty deep,
    And there should be her grave;
Nail to the mast her holy flag,
    Set every threadbare sail,
And give her to the god of storms,
    The lightning and the gale!

51   *The Deacon's Masterpiece:*

OR, THE WONDERFUL ONE-HOSS SHAY

A Logical Story

HAVE you heard of the wonderful one-hoss shay,
That was built in such a logical way
It ran a hundred years to a day,
And then of a sudden, it — ah, but stay,
I'll tell you what happened without delay,

Scaring the parson into fits,
Frightening people out of their wits, —
Have you ever heard of that, I say?

Seventeen hundred and fifty-five.
Georgius Secundus was then alive, —
Snuffy old drone from the German hive.
That was the year when Lisbon-town
Saw the earth open and gulp her down,
And Braddock's army was done so brown,
Left without a scalp to its crown.
It was on the terrible earthquake-day
That the Deacon finished the one-hoss shay.

Now in building of chaises, I tell you what,
There is always *somewhere* a weakest spot, —
In hub, tire, felloe, in spring or thill,
In panel, or crossbar, or floor, or sill,
In screw, bolt, thoroughbrace, — lurking still,
Find it somewhere you must and will, —
Above or below, or within or without, —
And that's the reason, beyond a doubt,
A chaise *breaks down*, but doesn't *wear out*.

But the Deacon swore (as Deacons do,
With an " I dew vum," or an " I tell *yeou*,")
He would build one shay to beat the taown
'n' the keounty 'n' all the kentry raoun' :
It should be so built that it *couldn'* break daown ;
— " Fur," said the Deacon, " 't's mighty plain
Thut the weakes' place mus' stan' the strain,
'n' the way t' fix it, uz I maintain,
   Is only jest
I' make that place uz strong uz the rest."

So the Deacon inquired of the village folk
Where he could find the strongest oak,
That couldn't be split nor bent nor broke, —
That was for spokes and floor and sills ;
He sent for lancewood to make the thills ;
The crossbars were ash, from the straightest
   trees ;
The panels of whitewood, that cuts like cheese
But lasts like iron for things like these ;
The hubs of logs from the " Settler's ellum," —
Last of its timber, — they couldn't sell 'em,
Never an axe had seen their chips,

And the wedges flew from between their lips,
Their blunt ends frizzled like celery-tips;
Step and prop-iron, bolt and screw,
Spring, tire, axle, and linchpin too,
Steel of the finest, bright and blue;
Thoroughbrace bison-skin, thick and wide;
Boot, top, dasher, from tough old hide
Found in the pit when the tanner died.
That was the way he " put her through."
" There!" said the Deacon, " naow she'll dew!

Do! I tell you, I rather guess
She was a wonder, and nothing less!
Colts grew horses, beards turned gray,
Deacon and deaconess dropped away,
Children and grandchildren, — where were they
But there stood the stout old one-hoss shay
As fresh as on Lisbon-earthquake-day!

EIGHTEEN HUNDRED; — it came and found
The Deacon's masterpiece strong and sound.
Eighteen hundred increased by ten; —
" Hahnsum kerridge" they called it then.

Eighteen hundred and twenty came; —
Running as usual; much the same.
Thirty and forty at last arrive,
And then came fifty, and FIFTY-FIVE.

Little of all we value here
Wakes on the morn of its hundredth year
Without both feeling and looking queer.
In fact, there's nothing that keeps its youth,
So far as I know, but a tree and truth.
(This is a moral that runs at large;
Take it. — You're welcome. — No extra charge.)

FIRST OF NOVEMBER, — the Earthquake-day. —
There are traces of age in the one-hoss shay,
A general flavor of mild decay,
But nothing local as one may say.
There couldn't be, — for the Deacon's art
Had made it so like in every part
That there wasn't a chance for one to start.
For the wheels were just as strong as the thills,
And the floor was just as strong as the sills,
And the panels just as strong as the floor,
And the whippletree neither less nor more,

And the back-crossbar as strong as the **fore,**
And spring and axle and hub *encore,*
And yet, *as a whole*, it is past a doubt
In another hour it will be *worn out !*

First of November, 'Fifty-five !
This morning the parson takes a **drive.**
Now, small boys, get out of the way !
Here comes the wonderful one-hoss **shay,**
Drawn by a rat-tailed, ewe-necked bay.
" Huddup ! " said the parson. — Off went they
The parson was working his Sunday's text, —
Had got to *fifthly,* and stopped perplexed
At what the — Moses — was coming next.
All at once the horse stood still,
Close by the meet'n'-house on the **hill.**
— First a shiver, and then a thrill,
Then something decidedly like a spill, —
And the parson was sitting upon a rock,
At half-past nine by the meet'n'-house **clock,** –
Just the hour of the Earthquake shock !
— What do you think the parson **found,**
When he got up and stared around ?

The poor old chaise in a heap or mound,
As if it had been to the mill and ground!
You see, of course, if you're not a dunce,
How it went to pieces all at once, —
All at once, and nothing first, —
Just as bubbles do when they burst.

End of the wonderful one-hoss shay.
Logic is logic.   That's all I say.

52   *The Voiceless*

WE count the broken lyres that rest
   Where the sweet wailing singers slumber, —
But o'er their silent sister's breast
   The wild flowers who will stoop to number?
A few can touch the magic string,
   And noisy Fame is proud to win them; —
Alas for those that never sing,
   But die with all their music in them!

Nay, grieve not for the dead alone
   Whose song has told their hearts' sad story, —

Weep for the voiceless, who have known
  The cross without the crown of glory!
Not where Leucadian breezes sweep
  O'er Sappho's memory-haunted billow,
But where the glistening night-dews weep
  On nameless sorrow's churchyard pillow

O hearts that break and give no sign
  Save whitening lip and fading tresses,
Till Death pours out his cordial wine
  Slow-dropped from Misery's crushing
    presses —
If singing breath or echoing chord
  To every hidden pang were given,
What endless melodies were poured,
  As sad as earth, as sweet as heaven!

ALFRED BILLINGS STREET

The Settler

53

His echoing axe the settler swung
    Amid the sea-like solitude,
And, rushing, thundering, down were flung
    The Titans of the wood;
Loud shrieked the eagle, as he dashed
From out his mossy nest, which crashed
    With its supporting bough,
And the first sunlight, leaping, flashed
    On the wolf's haunt below.

Rude was the garb and strong the frame
    Of him who plied his ceaseless toil:
To form that garb the wildwood game
    Contributed their spoil;
The soul that warmed that frame disdained
The tinsel, gaud, and glare that reigned
    Where men their crowds collect;

The simple fur, untrimmed, unstained,
   This forest-tamer decked.

The paths which wound mid gorgeous trees,
   The stream whose bright lips kissed their
      flowers,
The winds that swelled their harmonies
   Through those sun-hiding bowers,
The temple vast, the green arcade,
The nestling vale, the grassy glade,
   Dark cave, and swampy lair;
These scenes and sounds majestic made
   His world, his pleasures, there.

His roof adorned a pleasant spot;
   Mid the black logs green glowed the grain,
And herbs and plants the woods knew not
   Throve in the sun and rain.
The smoke-wreath curling o'er the dell,
The low, the bleat, the tinkling bell,
   All made a landscape strange,
Which was the living chronicle
   Of deeds that wrought the change.

The violet sprung at spring's first tinge,
   The rose of summer spread its glow,
The maize hung out its autumn fringe,
   Rude winter brought his snow;
And still the lone one labored there,
His shout and whistle broke the air,
   As cheerily he plied
His garden-spade, or drove his share
   Along the hillock's side.

He marked the fire-storm's blazing flood
   Roaring and crackling on its path,
And scorching earth, and melting wood,
   Beneath its greedy wrath;
He marked the rapid whirlwind shoot,
Trampling the pine-tree with its foot,
   And darkening thick the day
With streaming bough and severed root,
   Hurled whizzing on its way.

His gaunt hound yelled, his rifle flashed,
   The grim bear hushed his savage growl,
In blood and foam the panther gnashed
   His fangs, with dying howl;

The fleet deer ceased its flying bound,
Its snarling wolf-foe bit the ground,
    And, with its moaning cry,
The beaver sank beneath the wound
    Its pond-built Venice by.

Humble the lot, yet his the race,
    When Liberty sent forth her cry,
Who thronged in conflict's deadliest place,
    To fight, — to bleed, — to die !
Who cumbered Bunker's height of red,
By hope through weary years were led,
    And witnessed Yorktown's sun
Blaze on a nation's banner spread,
    A nation's freedom won.

FRANCES SARGENT OSGOOD

54

Labor

PAUSE not to dream of the future before us;
Pause not to weep the wild cares that come o'er
    us;
Hark, how Creation's deep, musical chorus,
  Unintermitting, goes up into heaven!
Never the ocean wave falters in flowing;
Never the little seed stops in its growing;
More and more richly the rose-heart keeps
    glowing,
  Till from its nourishing stem it is riven.

"Labor is worship!"—the robin is singing;
"Labor is worship!"—the wild bee is ringing;
Listen! that eloquent whisper, upspringing,
  Speaks to thy soul from out Nature's great
  heart.
From the dark cloud flows the life-giving
  shower;

From the rough sod blows the soft-breathing
    flower;
From the small insect, the rich coral bower;
    Only man in the plan shrinks from his part.

Labor is life! — 'tis the still water faileth;
Idleness ever despaireth, bewaileth;
Keep the watch wound, for the dark rust
    assaileth;
    Flowers droop and die in the stillness of
      noon.
Labor is glory! — the flying cloud lightens;
Only the waving wing changes and brightens;
Idle hearts only the dark future frightens;
    Play the sweet keys, wouldst thou keep them
      in tune!

Labor is rest, — from the sorrows that greet us;
Rest from all petty vexations that meet us;
Rest from sin-promptings that ever entreat us;
    Rest from world-sirens that lure us to ill.
Work, — and pure slumbers shall wait on thy
    pillow;

Work, — thou shalt ride over Care's coming
    billow :
Lie not down wearied 'neath Woe's weeping-
    willow !
    Work with a stout heart and resolute will !

Labor is health ! — Lo ! the husbandman reap-
    ing,
How through his veins goes the life-current
    leaping !
How his strong arm in his stalwart pride sweep-
    ing,
    True as a sunbeam the swift sickle guides.
Labor is wealth, — in the sea the pearl groweth ;
Rich the queen's robe from the frail cocoon
    floweth ;
From the fine acorn the strong forest bloweth ;
    Temple and statue the marble block hides.

Droop not, — though shame, sin, and anguish
    are round thee !
Bravely fling off the cold chain that hath bound
    thee !

Look to yon pure heaven smiling beyond thee!
    Rest not content in thy darkness, — a clod!
Work for some good, be it ever so slowly!
Cherish some flower, be it ever so lowly!
Labor! — all labor is noble and holy;
    Let thy great deeds be thy prayer to thy
    God.

HENRY THEODORE TUCKERMAN

55

To an Elm

BRAVELY thy old arms fling
Their countless pennons to the fields of air,
   And, like a sylvan king,
Their panoply of green still proudly wear.

   As some rude tower of old,
Their massive trunk still rears its rugged form
   With limbs of giant mould,
To battle sternly with the winter storm.

   In Nature's mighty fane,
Thou art the noblest arch beneath the sky;
   How long the pilgrim train
That with a benison have passed thee by!

   Lone patriarch of the wood!
Like a true spirit thou dost freely rise,
   Of fresh and dauntless mood,
Spreading thy branches to the open skies.

The locust knows thee well,
And when the summer days his notes prolong,
  Hid in some leafy cell,
Pours from thy world of green his drowsy song.

  Oft, on a morn in spring,
The yellow-bird will seek thy waving spray,
  And there securely swing,
To whet his beak, and pour his blithesome lay.

  How bursts thy monarch wail,
When sleeps the pulse of Nature's buoyant life,
  And, bared to meet the gale,
Wave thy old branches, eager for the strife!

  The sunset often weaves
Upon thy crest a wreath of splendor rare,
  While the fresh-murmuring leaves
Fill with cool sound the evening's sultry air.

  Sacred thy roof of green
To rustic dance, and childhood's gambols free;
  Gay youth and age serene
Turn with familiar gladness unto thee.

Oh, hither should we roam,
To hear Truth's herald in the lofty shade;
　Beneath thy emerald dome
Might Freedom's champion fitly draw his blade.

　With blessings at thy feet,
Falls the worn peasant to his noontide rest;
　Thy verdant, calm retreat
Inspires the sad and soothes the troubled breast.

　When, at the twilight hour,
Plays through thy tressil crown the sun's last
　　gleam,
　Under thy ancient bower
The schoolboy comes to sport, the bard to dream.

　And when the moonbeams fall
Through thy broad canopy upon the grass,
　Making a fairy hall,
As o'er the sward the flitting shadows pass —

　Then lovers haste to thee,
With hearts that tremble like that shifting light;
　To them, O brave old tree,
Thou art Joy's shrine — a temple of delight!

CHRISTOPHER PEARSE CRANCH

56

The Bobolinks

WHEN Nature had made all her birds,
 With no more cares to think on,
She gave a rippling laugh, and out
 There flew a Bobolinkon.

She laughed again; out flew a mate;
 A breeze of Eden bore them
Across the fields of Paradise,
 The sunrise reddening o'er them.

Incarnate sport and holiday,
 They flew and sang forever;
Their souls through June were all in tune
 Their wings were weary never.

Their tribe, still drunk with air and light,
 And perfume of the meadow,
Go reeling up and down the sky,
 In sunshine and in shadow.

One springs from out the dew-wet grass;
  Another follows after;
The morn is thrilling with their songs
  And peals of fairy laughter.

From out the marshes and the brook,
  They set the tall reeds swinging,
And meet and frolic in the air,
  Half prattling and half singing.

When morning winds sweep meadow-lands
  In green and russet billows,
And toss the lonely elm-tree's boughs,
  And silver all the willows,

I see you buffeting the breeze,
  Or with its motion swaying,
Your notes half drowned against the wind,
  Or down the current playing.

When far away o'er grassy flats,
  Where the thick wood commences,
The white-sleeved mowers look like specks
  Beyond the zigzag fences,

And noon is hot, and barn-roofs gleam
    White in the pale blue distance,
I hear the saucy minstrels still
    In chattering persistence.

When Eve her domes of opal fire
    Piles round the blue horizon,
Or thunder rolls from hill to hill
    A Kyrie Eleison,

Still merriest of the merry birds,
    Your sparkle is unfading, —
Pied harlequins of June, — no end
    Of song and masquerading.

What cadences of bubbling mirth,
    Too quick for bar and rhythm!
What ecstasies, too full to keep
    Coherent measure with them!

O could I share, without champagne
    Or muscadel, your frolic,
The glad delirium of your joy,
    Your fun unapostolic,

Your drunken jargon through the fields,
    Your bobolinkish gabble,
Your fine Anacreontic glee,
    Your tipsy reveller's babble!

Nay, let me not profane such joy
    With similes of folly;
No wine of earth could waken songs
    So delicately jolly!

O boundless self-contentment, voiced
    In flying air-born bubbles!
O joy that mocks our sad unrest,
    And drowns our earth-born troubles!

Hope springs with you: I dread no more
    Despondency and dulness;
For Good Supreme can never fail
    That gives such perfect fulness.

The life that floods the happy fields
    With song and light and color
Will shape our lives to richer states,
    And heap our measures fuller.

HARRIET BEECHER STOWE

Only a Year

ONE year ago, — a ringing voice,
    A clear blue eye,
And clustering curls of sunny hair,
    Too fair to die.

Only a year, — no voice, no smile,
    No glance of eye,
No clustering curls of golden hair,
    Fair but to die!

One year ago, — what loves, what schemes
    Far into life!
What joyous hopes, what high resolves,
    What generous strife!

The silent picture on the wall,
    The burial-stone
Of all that beauty, life, and joy,
    Remain alone!

One year, — one year, — one little **year,**
    And so much gone!
And yet the even flow of life
    Moves calmly on.

The grave grows green, the flowers bloom **fair,**
    Above that head;
No sorrowing tint of leaf or spray
    Says he is dead.

No pause or hush of merry **birds**
    That sing above
Tells us how coldly sleeps **below**
    The form we love.

Where hast thou been this year, **beloved?**
    What hast thou seen, —
What visions fair, what glorious **life,**
    Where thou hast been?

The veil! the veil! so thin, so **strong!**
    'Twixt us and thee;
The mystic veil! when shall it **fall,**
    That we may see?

Not dead, not sleeping, not even gone,
  But present still,
And waiting for the coming hour
  Of God's sweet will.

Lord of the living and the dead,
  Our Saviour dear!
We lay in silence at thy feet
  This sad, sad year.

PHILIP PENDLETON COOKE

58   *Life in the Autumn Woods*

[VIRGINIA]

SUMMER has gone,
And fruitful Autumn has advanced so far
That there is warmth, not heat, in the broad
    sun,
And you may look, with naked eye, upon
    The ardors of his car;
The stealthy frosts, whom his spent looks em-
    bolden,
    Are making the green leaves golden.

What a brave splendor
Is in the October air! how rich, and clear,
And bracing, and all-joyous! We must render
Love to the Spring-time, with its sproutings
    tender,
    As to a child quite dear;

But Autumn is a thing of perfect glory,
      A manhood not yet hoary.

      I love the woods,
In this good season of the liberal year;
I love to seek their leafy solitudes,
And give myself to melancholy moods,
      With no intruder near,
And find strange lessons, as I sit and ponder,
      In every natural wonder.

      But not alone,
As Shakespeare's melancholy courtier loved
      Ardennes,
Love I the browning forest; and I own
I would not oft have mused, as he, but flown
      To hunt with Amiens —
And little thought, as up the bold deer bounded,
      Of the sad creature wounded.

      A brave and good,
But world-worn knight — soul-wearied with his
      part
In this vexed life — gave man for solitude,

And built a lodge, and lived in Wantley wood,
  To hear the belling hart.
It was a gentle taste, but its sweet sadness
  Yields to the hunter's madness.

  What passionate
And keen delight is in the proud swift chase!
Go out what time the lark at heaven's red gate
Soars joyously singing — quite infuriate
  With the high pride of his place;
What time the unrisen sun arrays the morning
  In its first bright adorning.

  Hark! the quick horn —
As sweet to hear as any clarion —
Piercing with silver call the ear of morn;
And mark the steeds, stout Curtal and Top
  thorne,
  And Greysteil and the Don —
Each one of them his fiery mood displaying
  With pawing and with neighing.

  Urge your swift horse
After the crying hounds in this fresh hour;

Vanquish high hills, stem perilous streams per-
    force,
On the free plain give free wings to your
    course,
      And you will know the power
Of the brave chase, — and how of griefs the
    sorest
      A cure is in the forest.

      Or stalk the deer;
The same red lip of dawn has kissed the hills,
The gladdest sounds are crowding on your ear,
There is a life in all the atmosphere : —
      Your very nature fills
With the fresh hour, as up the hills aspiring
      You climb with limbs untiring.

      It is a fair
And goodly sight to see the antlered stag
With the long sweep of his swift walk repair
To join his brothers ; or the plethoric bear
      Lying in some high crag,

With pinky eyes half closed, but broad head
    shaking,
        As gadflies keep him waking.

    And these you see,
And, seeing them, you travel to their death
With a slow, stealthy step, from tree to tree,
Noting the wind, however faint it be.
        The hunter draws a breath
In times like these, which, he will say, repays
    him
        For all care that waylays him.

    A strong joy fills
(A joy beyond the tongue's expressive power)
My heart in Autumn weather — fills and thrills!
And I would rather stalk the breezy hills
        Descending to my bower
Nightly, by the sweet spirit of Peace attended,
        Than pine where life is splendid.

EMILY CHUBBUCK JUDSON

59

Watching

SLEEP, love, sleep!
The dusty day is done.
Lo! from afar the freshening breezes sweep
Wide over groves of balm,
Down from the towering palm,
In at the open casement cooling run,
And round thy lowly bed,
Thy bed of pain,
Bathing thy patient head,
Like grateful showers of rain,
They come;
While the white curtains, waving to and fro
Fan the sick air;
And pityingly the shadows come and go,
With gentle human care,
Compassionate and dumb.

The dusty day is done,
The night begun ;
While prayerful watch I keep,
Sleep, love, sleep !
Is there no magic in the touch
Of fingers thou dost love so much ?
Fain would they scatter poppies o'er thee now ;
Or, with its mute caress,
The tremulous lip some soft nepenthe press
Upon thy weary lid and aching brow ;
While prayerful watch I keep,
Sleep, love, sleep !

On the pagoda spire
The bells are swinging,
Their little golden circlet in a flutter
With tales the wooing winds have dared to
    utter,
Till all are ringing,
As if a choir
Of golden-nested birds in heaven were singing,
And with a lulling sound
The music floats around,

And drops like balm into the drowsy ear;
Commingling with the hum
Of the Sepoy's distant drum,
And lazy beetle ever droning near.
Sounds these of deepest silence born,
Like night made visible by morn;
So silent that I sometimes start
To hear the throbbings of my heart,
And watch, with shivering sense of pain,
To see thy pale lids lift again.

The lizard, with his mouse-like eyes,
Peeps from the mortise in surprise
At such strange quiet after day's harsh din;
Then boldly ventures out,
And looks about,
And with his hollow feet
Treads his small evening beat,
Darting upon his prey
In such a tricky, winsome sort of way.
His delicate marauding seems no sin.
And still the curtains swing,
But noiselessly;

The bells a melancholy murmur ring,
As tears were in the sky:
More heavily the shadows fall,
Like the black foldings of a pall,
Where juts the rough beam from the wall:
The candles flare
With fresher gusts of air:
The beetle's drone
Turns to a dirge-like, solitary moan;
Night deepens, and I sit, in cheerless doubt
    alone.

JOSIAH GILBERT HOLLAND

60

Cradle Song

FROM "BITTER SWEET"

WHAT is the little one thinking about?
Very wonderful things, no doubt;
      Unwritten history!
      Unfathomed mystery!
Yet he laughs and cries, and eats and drinks,
And chuckles, and crows, and nods, and winks,
As if his head were as full of kinks
And curious riddles as any sphinx!
   Warped by colic, and wet by tears,
   Punctured by pins, and tortured by fears,
   Our little nephew will lose two years;
      And he'll never know
      Where the summers go; —
He need not laugh, for he'll find it so.

Who can tell what a baby thinks?
Who can follow the gossamer links
      By which the manikin feels his way

Out from the shore of the great unknown,
Blind, and wailing, and alone,
  Into the light of day ? —
Out from the shore of the unknown sea,
Tossing in pitiful agony, —
Of the unknown sea that reels and rolls,
Specked with the barks of little souls —
Barks that were launched on the other side,
And slipped from heaven on an ebbing tide !
  What does he think of his mother's eyes?
What does he think of his mother's hair?
  What of the cradle-roof, that flies
Forward and backward through the air?
  What does he think of his mother's breast —
Bare and beautiful, smooth and white,
Seeking it ever with fresh delight —
  Cup of his life, and couch of his rest?
What does he think when her quick embrace
Presses his hand and buries his face
Deep where the heart-throbs sink and swell,
With a tenderness she can never tell,
  Though she murmur the words
  Of all the birds —

Words she has learned to murmur well?
  Now he thinks he'll go to sleep!
  I can see the shadow creep
  Over his eyes in soft eclipse,
  Over his brow and over his lips,
  Out to his little finger-tips!
  Softly sinking, down he goes!
  Down he goes! down he goes!
  See! he's hushed in sweet repose.

HARRIET WINSLOW SEWALL

61

Why thus Longing?

WHY thus longing, thus forever sighing,
  For the far-off, unattained and dim,
While the beautiful, all round thee lying,
  Offers up its low, perpetual hymn?

Would'st thou listen to its gentle teaching,
  All thy restless yearnings it would still;
Leaf and flower and laden bee are preaching
  Thine own sphere, though humble, first to fill.

Poor indeed thou must be, if around thee
  Thou no ray of light and joy canst throw —
If no silken cord of love hath bound thee
  To some little world through weal and woe;

If no dear eyes thy fond love can brighten —
  No fond voices answer to thine own;
If no brother's sorrow thou canst lighten,
  By daily sympathy and gentle tone.

Not by deeds that gain the world's applauses,
   Not by works that win thee world-renown,
Not by martyrdom or vaunted crosses,
   Canst thou win and wear the immortal crown!

Daily struggling, though unloved and lonely,
   Every day a rich reward will give;
Thou wilt find, by hearty striving only,
   And truly loving, thou canst truly live.

Dost thou revel in the rosy morning,
   When all nature hails the lord of light,
And his smile, the mountain tops adorning,
   Robes yon fragrant fields in radiance bright?

Other hands may grasp the field and forest,
   Proud proprietors in pomp may shine;
But with fervent love if thou adorest,
   Thou art wealthier — all the world is thine.

Yet if through earth's wide domains thou rovest,
   Sighing that they are not thine alone,
Not those fair fields, but thyself, thou lovest,
   And their beauty and thy wealth are gone.

Nature wears the color of the spirit;
  Sweetly to her worshipper she sings;
All the glow, the grace she doth inherit,
  Round her trusting child she fondly flings.

JAMES RUSSELL LOWELL

62

To the Dandelion

DEAR common flower, that grow'st beside the
  way,
Fringing the dusty road with harmless gold,
    First pledge of blithesome May,
Which children pluck, and, full of pride, uphold,
  High-hearted buccaneers, o'erjoyed that they
An Eldorado in the grass have found,
Which not the rich earth's ample round
  May match in wealth, — thou art more dear
    to me
  Than all the prouder summer-blooms may be.

Gold such as thine ne'er drew the Spanish
  prow
Through the primeval hush of Indian seas,
    Nor wrinkled the lean brow
Of age, to rob the lover's heart of ease;
  'Tis the spring's largess, which she scatters
    now

To rich and poor alike, with lavish hand,
Though most hearts never understand
   To take it at God's value, but pass by
   The offered wealth with unrewarded eye.

   Thou art my tropics and mine Italy;
To look at thee unlocks a warmer clime;
     The eyes thou givest me
Are in the heart, and heed not space or time:
   Not in mid June the golden-cuirassed bee
Feels a more summer-like warm ravishment
In the white lily's breezy tent,
   His fragrant Sybaris, than I, when first
   From the dark green thy yellow circles burst

   Then think I of deep shadows on the grass, —
Of meadows where in sun the cattle graze,
     Where, as the breezes pass,
The gleaming rushes lean a thousand ways, —
   Of leaves that slumber in a cloudy mass,
Or whiten in the wind, — of waters blue
That from the distance sparkle through

Some woodland gap, — and of a sky above,
Where one white cloud like a stray lamb doth
    move.

My childhood's earliest thoughts are linked
    with thee;
The sight of thee calls back the robin's song,
        Who, from the dark old tree
Beside the door, sang clearly all day long,
    And I, secure in childish piety,
Listened as if I heard an angel sing
With news from heaven, which he could bring
    Fresh every day to my untainted ears,
        When birds and flowers and I were happy
        peers.

How like a prodigal doth nature seem,
When thou, for all thy gold, so common art!
        Thou teachest me to deem
More sacredly of every human heart,
    Since each reflects in joy its scanty gleam
Of heaven, and could some wondrous secret show
Did we but pay the love we owe,
    And with a child's undoubting wisdom look
    On all these living pages of God's book.

63   *Rhœcus*

GOD sends his teachers unto every age,
To every clime, and every race of men,
With revelations fitted to their growth
And shape of mind, nor gives the realm of
        Truth
Into the selfish rule of one sole race:
Therefore each form of worship that hath
        swayed
The life of man, and given it to grasp
The master-key of knowledge, reverence,
Enfolds some germs of goodness and of right;
Else never had the eager soul, which loathes
The slothful down of pampered ignorance,
Found in it even a moment's fitful rest.

There is an instinct in the human heart
Which makes that all the fables it hath coined,
To justify the reign of its belief
And strengthen it by beauty's right divine,
Veil in their inner cells a mystic gift,
Which, like the hazel twig, in faithful hands,

Points surely to the hidden springs of truth.
For, as in nature naught is made in vain,
But all things have within their hull of use
A wisdom and a meaning which may speak
Of spiritual secrets to the ear
Of spirit; so, in whatsoe'er the heart
Hath fashioned for solace to itself,
To make its inspirations suit its creed,
And from the niggard hands of falsehood wring
Its needful food of truth, there ever is
A sympathy with Nature, which reveals,
Not less than her own works, pure gleams of
    light
And earnest parables of inward lore.
Hear now this fairy legend of old Greece,
As full of freedom, youth, and beauty still
As the immortal freshness of that grace
Carved for all ages on some Attic frieze.

  A youth named Rhœcus, wandering in the
    wood,
Saw an old oak just trembling to its fall,
And, feeling pity of so fair a tree,
He propped its gray trunk with admiring care.

And with a thoughtless footstep loitered on.
But, as he turned, he heard a voice behind
That murmured "Rhœcus!" 'Twas as if the
    leaves,
Stirred by a passing breath, had murmured it,
And, while he paused bewildered, yet again
It murmured "Rhœcus!" softer than a breeze.
He started and beheld with dizzy eyes
What seemed the substance of a happy dream
Stand there before him, spreading a warm glow
Within the green glooms of the shadowy oak.
It seemed a woman's shape, yet all too fair
To be a woman, and with eyes too meek
For any that were wont to mate with gods.
All naked like a goddess stood she there,
And like a goddess all too beautiful
To feel the guilt-born earthliness of shame.
" Rhœcus, I am the Dryad of this tree,"
Thus she began, dropping her low-toned words
Serene, and full, and clear, as drops of dew,
" And with it I am doomed to live and die;
The rain and sunshine are my caterers,
Nor have I other bliss than simple life;

Now ask me what thou wilt, that I can give,
And with a thankful joy it shall be thine."

Then Rhœcus, with a flutter at the heart,
Yet, by the prompting of such beauty, bold,
Answered: "What is there that can satisfy
The endless craving of the soul but love?
Give me thy love, or but the hope of that
Which must be evermore my spirit's goal."
After a little pause she said again,
But with a glimpse of sadness in her tone,
"I give it, Rhœcus, though a perilous gift;
An hour before the sunset meet me here."
And straightway there was nothing he could see
But the green glooms beneath the shadowy oak,
And not a sound came to his straining ears
But the low trickling rustle of the leaves,
And far away upon an emerald slope
The falter of an idle shepherd's pipe.

Now, in those days of simpleness and faith,
Men did not think that happy things were
    dreams
Because they overstepped the narrow bourne

Of likelihood, but reverently deemed
Nothing too wondrous or too beautiful
To be the guerdon of a daring heart.
So Rhœcus made no doubt that he was blest,
And all along unto the city's gate
Earth seemed to spring beneath him as he
        walked,
The clear, broad sky looked bluer than its wont,
And he could scarce believe he had not wings
Such sunshine seemed to glitter through his veins
Instead of blood, so light he felt and strange.

Young Rhœcus had a faithful heart enough,
But one that in the present dwelt too much,
And, taking with blithe welcome whatsoe'er
Chance gave of joy, was wholly bound in that,
Like the contented peasant of a vale,
Deemed it the world, and never looked beyond.
So, haply meeting in the afternoon
Some comrades who were playing at the dice,
He joined them and forgot all else beside.

The dice were rattling at the merriest,
And Rhœcus, who had met but sorry luck,

Just laughed in triumph at a happy throw,
When through the room there hummed a yellow
    bee
That buzzed about his ear with down-dropped
    legs
As if to light.   And Rhœcus laughed and said,
Feeling how red and flushed he was with loss,
" By Venus! does he take me for a rose ? "
And brushed him off with rough, impatient
    hand.
But still the bee came back, and thrice again
Rhœcus did beat him off with growing wrath.
Then through the window flew the wounded
    bee,
And Rhœcus, tracking him with angry eyes,
Saw a sharp mountain-peak of Thessaly
Against the red disk of the setting sun, —
And instantly the blood sank from his heart,
As if its very walls had caved away.
Without a word he turned, and, rushing forth,
Ran madly through the city and the gate,
And o'er the plain, which now the wood's long
    shade.

By the low sun thrown forward broad and dim,
Darkened well-nigh unto the city's wall.
  Quite spent and out of breath he reached the
      tree,
And, listening fearfully, he heard once more
The low voice murmur "Rhœcus!" close at
      hand:
Whereat he looked around him, but could see
Naught but the deepening glooms beneath the
      oak.
Then sighed the voice, "Oh, Rhœcus! never-
      more
Shalt thou behold me or by day or night,
Me, who would fain have blessed thee with a
      love
More ripe and bounteous than ever yet
Filled up with nectar any mortal heart:
But thou didst scorn my humble messenger,
And sent'st him back to me with bruisèd
      wings.
We spirits only show to gentle eyes.
We ever ask an undivided love,
And he who scorns the least of Nature's works

Is thenceforth exiled and shut out from all.
Farewell! for thou canst never see me more."

   Then Rhœcus beat his breast, and groaned
     aloud
And cried, "Be pitiful! forgive me yet
This once, and I shall never need it more!"
"Alas!" the voice returned, "'tis thou art
     blind,
Not I unmerciful; I can forgive,
But have no skill to heal thy spirit's eyes;
Only the soul hath power o'er itself."
With that again there murmured "Nevermore!"
And Rhœcus after heard no other sound,
Except the rattling of the oak's crisp leaves,
Like the long surf upon a distant shore,
Raking the sea-worn pebbles up and down.
The night had gathered round him: o'er the
     plain
The city sparkled with its thousand lights,
And sounds of revel fell upon his ear
Harshly and like a curse; above, the sky,
With all its bright sublimity of stars.

Deepened, and on his forehead smote the breeze;
Beauty was all around him and delight,
But from that eve he was alone on earth.

64   *The Present Crisis*

WHEN a deed is done for Freedom, through the
          broad earth's aching breast
Runs a thrill of joy prophetic, trembling on
          from east to west,
And the slave, where'er he cowers, feels the
          soul within him climb
To the awful verge of manhood, as the energy
          sublime
Of a century bursts full-blossomed on the
          thorny stem of Time.

Through the walls of hut and palace shoots the
          instantaneous throe,
When the travail of the Ages wrings earth's
          systems to and fro;
At the birth of each new Era, with a recogniz-
          ing start,

Nation wildly looks at nation, standing with
    mute lips apart,
And glad Truth's yet mightier man-child leaps
    beneath the Future's heart.

So the Evil's triumph sendeth, with a terror
    and a chill,
Under continent to continent, the sense of
    coming ill,
And the slave, where'er he cowers, feels his
    sympathies with God
In hot tear-drops ebbing earthward, to be drunk
    up by the sod,
Till a corpse crawls round unburied, delving
    in the nobler clod.

For mankind are one in spirit, and an instinct
    bears along,
Round the earth's electric circle, the swift flush
    of right or wrong;
Whether conscious or unconscious, yet Human-
    ity's vast frame

Through its ocean-sundered fibres feels the
    gush of joy or shame; —
In the gain or loss of one race all the rest have
    equal claim.

Once to every man and nation comes the mo-
    ment to decide,
In the strife of Truth with Falsehood, for the
    good or evil side;
Some great cause, God's new Messiah, offering
    each the bloom or blight,
Parts the goats upon the left hand, and the
    sheep upon the right,
And the choice goes by forever 'twixt that
    darkness and that light.

Hast thou chosen, O my people, on whose
    party thou shalt stand,
Ere the Doom from its worn sandals shakes
    the dust against our land?
Though the cause of Evil prosper, yet 'tis
    Truth alone is strong,

And, albeit she wander outcast now, I see
    around her throng
Troops of beautiful, tall angels, to enshield her
    from all wrong.

Backward look across the ages and the beacon-
    moments see,
That, like peaks of some sunk continent, jut
    through Oblivion's sea;
Not an ear in court or market for the low fore-
    boding cry
Of those Crises, God's stern winnowers, from
    whose feet earth's chaff must fly;
Never shows the choice momentous till the
    judgment hath passed by.

Careless seems the great Avenger; history's
    pages but record
One death-grapple in the darkness 'twixt old
    systems and the Word;
Truth forever on the scaffold, Wrong forever
    on the throne, —

Yet that scaffold sways the Future, and, behind
    the dim unknown,
Standeth God within the shadow, keeping
    watch above his own.

We see dimly in the Present what is small and
    what is great,
Slow of faith, how weak an arm may turn the
    iron helm of fate,
But the soul is still oracular; amid the market's
    din,
List the ominous stern whisper from the Del-
    phic cave within, —
"They enslave their children's children who
    make compromise with sin."

Slavery, the earthborn Cyclops, fellest of the
    giant brood,
Sons of brutish Force and Darkness, who have
    drenched the earth with blood,
Famished in his self-made desert, blinded by
    our purer day,

Gropes in yet unblasted regions for his misera‧
    ble prey; —
Shall we guide his gory fingers where our help‧
    less children play?

Then to side with Truth is noble when we
    share her wretched crust,
Ere her cause bring fame and profit, and 'tis
    prosperous to be just;
Then it is the brave man chooses, while the
    coward stands aside,
Doubting in his abject spirit, till his Lord is
    crucified,
And the multitude make virtue of the faith
    they had denied.

Count me o'er earth's chosen heroes, — they
    were souls that stood alone,
While the men they agonized for hurled the
    contumelious stone,
Stood serene, and down the future saw the
    golden beam incline

To the side of perfect justice, mastered by their
    faith divine,
By one man's plain truth to manhood and to
    God's supreme design.

By the light of burning heretics Christ's bleed-
    ing feet I track,
Toiling up new Calvaries ever with the cross
    that turns not back,
And these mounts of anguish number how each
    generation learned
One new word of that grand *Credo* which in
    prophet-hearts hath burned
Since the first man stood God-conquered with
    his face to heaven upturned.

For Humanity sweeps onward: where to day
    the martyr stands,
On the morrow crouches Judas with the silver
    in his hands;
Far in front the cross stands ready and the
    crackling fagots burn,

While the hooting mob of yesterday in silent
    awe return
To glean up the scattered ashes into History's
    golden urn.

'Tis as easy to be heroes as to sit the idle
    slaves
Of a legendary virtue carved upon our fathers'
    graves,
Worshippers of light ancestral make the pres-
    ent light a crime; —
Was the Mayflower launched by cowards,
    steered by men behind their time?
Turn those tracks toward Past or Future, that
    make Plymouth rock sublime?

They were men of present valor, stalwart old
    iconoclasts,
Unconvinced by axe or gibbet that all virtue
    was the Past's;
But we make their truth our falsehood, thinking
    that hath made us free,

Hoarding it in mouldy parchments, while our
    tender spirits flee
The rude grasp of that great Impulse which
    drove them across the sea.

They have rights who dare maintain them; we
    are traitors to our sires,
Smothering in their holy ashes Freedom's new-
    lit altar-fires;
Shall we make their creed our jailer? Shall
    we, in our haste to slay,
From the tombs of the old prophets steal the
    funeral lamps away
To light up the martyr-fagots round the proph-
    ets of to-day?

New occasions teach new duties; Time makes
    ancient good uncouth;
They must upward still, and onward, who
    would keep abreast of Truth;
Lo, before us gleam her camp-fires! we our-
    selves must Pilgrims be,

Launch our Mayflower, and steer boldly
    through the desperate winter sea,
Nor attempt the Future's portal with the Past's
    blood-rusted key.

December, 1845.

65   *She Came and Went*

    As a twig trembles, which a bird
        Lights on to sing, then leaves unbent,
    So is my memory thrilled and stirred ; —
        I only know she came and went.

    As clasps some lake, by gusts unriven,
        The blue dome's measureless content,
    So my soul held that moment's heaven ; —
        I only know she came and went.

    As, at one bound, our swift spring heaps
        The orchards full of bloom and scent,
    So clove her May my wintry sleeps ; —
        I only know she came and went.

    An angel stood and met my gaze,
        Through the low doorway of my tent ;

The tent is struck, the vision stays; —
I only know she came and went.

O, when the room grows slowly dim,
And life's last oil is nearly spent,
One gush of light these eyes will brim,
Only to think she came and went.

WALT WHITMAN

66   *What is the Grass?*

FROM "WALT WHITMAN"

A CHILD said, *What is the grass?* fetching it to
    me with full hands;
How could I answer the child?   I do not know
    what it is, any more than he.

I guess it must be the flag of my disposition,
    out of hopeful green stuff woven.

Or I guess it is the handkerchief of the Lord,
A scented gift and remembrancer, designedly
    dropped,
Bearing the owner's name someway in the cor-
    ners, that we may see and remark, and say
    Whose?

Or I guess the grass is itself a child, the
    produced babe of the vegetation.

Or I guess it is a uniform hieroglyphic,
And it means, Sprouting alike in broad zones
   and narrow zones,
Growing among black folks as among white,
Kanuck, Tuckahoe, Congressman, Cuff, I give
   them the same, I receive them the same.

And now it seems to me the beautiful uncut
   hair of graves.

Tenderly will I use you, curling grass,
It may be you transpire from the breasts of
   young men,
It may be if I had known them I would have
   loved them,
It may be you are from old people, and from
   women, and from offspring taken soon out
   of their mothers' laps,
And here you are the mothers' laps.

This grass is very dark to be from the white
   heads of old mothers,
Darker than the colorless beards of old men,
Dark to come from under the faint red roofs ot
   mouths.

O I perceive after all so many uttering tongues!
And I perceive they do not come from the roofs
of mouths for nothing.

I wish I could translate the hints about the dead
young men and women,
And the hints about old men and mothers, and
the offspring taken soon out of their laps.

What do you think has become of the young
and old men?
And what do you think has become of the
women and children?

They are alive and well somewhere,
The smallest sprout shows there is really no
death,
And if ever there was, it led forward life, and
does not wait at the end to arrest it,
And ceased the moment life appeared.

All goes onward and outward — nothing col-
lapses,
And to die is different from what any one supposed, and luckier.

Has any one supposed it lucky to be born?
I hasten to inform him or her, it is just as lucky
　　to die, and I know it.

I pass death with the dying, and birth with the
　　new-washed babe, and am not contained
　　between my hat and boots,
And peruse manifold objects, no two alike, and
　　every one good,
The earth good, and the stars good, and their
　　adjuncts all good.

I am not an earth, nor an adjunct of an earth,
I am the mate and companion of people, all just
　　as immortal and fathomless as myself;
They do not know how immortal, but I know.

*　　*　　*　　*　　*　　*　　*

In all people I see myself — none more, and not
　　one a barleycorn less,
And the good or bad I say of myself I say of
　　them.

And I know I am solid and sound,
To me the converging objects of the universe
    perpetually flow,
All are written to me, and I must get what the
    writing means.

I know I am deathless,
I know this orbit of mine cannot be swept by a
    carpenter's compass,
I know I shall not pass like a child's carlacue
    cut with a burnt stick at night.

*   *   *   *   *   *   *

My foothold is tenoned and mortised in granite,
I laugh at what you call dissolution,
And I know the amplitude of time.

*   *   *   *   *   *   *

I open my scuttle at night and see the far
    sprinkled systems,
And all I see, multiplied as high as I can cipher,
    edge but the rim of the farther systems.

Wider and wider they spread, expanding, always
   expanding,
Outward, outward, and forever outward.

My sun has his sun, and round him obediently
   wheels,
He joins with his partners a group of superior
   circuit,
And greater sets follow, making specks of the
   greatest inside them.

There is no stoppage, and never can be stoppage,
If I, you, the worlds, all beneath or upon their
   surfaces, and all the palpable life, were this
   moment reduced back to a pallid float, it
   would not avail in the long run,
We should surely bring up again where we now
   stand,
And as surely go as much farther — and then
   farther and farther.

A few quadrillions of eras, a few octillions of
   cubic leagues, do not hazard the span, or
   make it impatient,
They are but parts — anything is but a part.

See ever so far, there is limitless space outside
of that,
Count ever so much, there is limitless time
around that.

My rendezvous is appointed,
The Lord will be there, and wait till I come on
perfect terms.

J know I have the best of time and space, and
was never measured, and never will be
measured.

67   *O Captain! my Captain!* [1]

O CAPTAIN! my Captain! our fearful trip is
done,
The ship has weathered every rack, the prize
we sought is won,
The port is near, the bells I hear, the people all
exulting,
While follow eyes the steady keel, the vessel
grim and daring;

[1] On the death of Abraham Lincoln.

But O heart ! heart ! heart !
 O the bleeding drops of red,
  Where on the deck my Captain lies,
   Fallen cold and dead.

O Captain ! my Captain ! rise up and hear the
 bells ;
Rise up — for you the flag is flung — for you
 the bugle trills,
For you bouquets and ribboned wreaths — for
 you the shores acrowding,
For you they call, the swaying mass, their eager
 faces turning ;
 Here Captain ! dear father !
  This arm beneath your head !
   It is some dream that on the deck
    You've fallen cold and dead.

My Captain does not answer, his lips are pale
 and still,
My father does not feel my arm, he has no
 pulse nor will,
The ship is anchored safe and sound, its voyage
 closed and done,

From fearful trip the victor ship comes in with
    object won;
  Exult O shores, and ring O bells!
    But I, with mournful tread,
      Walk the deck my Captain lies,
        Fallen cold and dead.

68   *Give me the Splendid Silent Sun*

GIVE me the splendid silent sun with all his
    beams full-dazzling,
Give me juicy autumnal fruit ripe and red from
    the orchard,
Give me a field where the unmowed grass
    grows,
Give me an arbor, give me the trellised grape,
Give me fresh corn and wheat, give me serene-
    moving animals teaching content,
Give me nights perfectly quiet as on high
    plateaus west of the Mississippi, and I look-
    ing up at the stars,
Give me odorous at sunrise a garden of beauti-
    ful flowers where I can walk undisturbed,

Give me for marriage a sweet-breathed woman
    of whom I should never tire,
Give me a perfect child, give me, away aside
    from the noise of the world, a rural domes-
    tic life,
Give me to warble spontaneous songs recluse by
    myself, for my own ears only,
Give me solitude, give me Nature, give me again
    O Nature your primal sanities!

These demanding to have them, (tired with
    ceaseless excitement, and racked by the
    war-strife)
These to procure incessantly asking, rising in
    cries from my heart,
While yet incessantly asking still I adhere to
    my city,
Day upon day and year upon year, O city,
    walking your streets,
Where you hold me enchained a certain time
    refusing to give me up,
Yet giving to make me glutted, enriched of soul,
    you give me forever faces;

(O I see what I sought to escape, confronting,
    reversing my cries,
I see my own soul trampling down what it
    asked for.)

Keep your splendid silent sun,
Keep your woods, O Nature, and the quiet
    places by the woods,
Keep your fields of clover and timothy, and
    your corn-fields and orchards,
Keep the blossoming buckwheat fields where
    the Ninth-month bees hum;
Give me faces and streets — give me these
    phantoms incessant and endless along the
    trottoirs!
Give me interminable eyes — give me women —
    give me comrades and lovers by the
    thousand!

Let me see new ones every day — let me hold
    new ones by the hand every day!
Give me such shows — give me the streets of
    Manhattan!

Give me Broadway, with the soldiers marching —
    give me the sound of the trumpets and
    drums !
(The soldiers in companies or regiments — some
    starting away flushed and reckless,
Some, their time up, returning with thinned
    ranks, young, yet very old, worn, marching
    noticing nothing ;)
Give me the shores and wharves heavy-fringed
    with black ships !
O such for me ! O an intense life, full to
    repletion and varied !
The life of the theatre, bar-room, huge hotel for
    me !
The saloon of the steamer ! The crowded
    excursion for me ! The torchlight proces-
    sion !
The dense brigade bound for the war, with high-
    piled military wagons following ;
People, endless, streaming, with strong voices,
    passions, pageants,
Manhattan streets with their powerful throbs,
    with beating drums as now,

The endless and noisy chorus, the rustle and
  clank of muskets (even the sight of the
  wounded),
Manhattan crowds, with their turbulent musical
  chorus!
Manhattan faces and eyes forever for me.

WILLIAM WETMORE STORY

69   *The Violet*

O FAINT, delicious, spring-time violet!
    Thine odor, like a key,
Turns noiselessly in memory's wards to let
    A thought of sorrow free.

The breath of distant fields upon my brow
    Blows through that open door
The sound of wind-borne bells, more sweet and
    low,
    And sadder than of yore.

It comes afar, from that belovèd place,
    And that belovèd hour,
When life hung ripening in love's golden grace,
    Like grapes above a bower.

A spring goes singing through its reedy grass,
    The lark sings o'er my head,

Drowned in the sky — O, pass, ye visions, pass!
  I would that I were dead! —

Why hast thou opened that forbidden door
  From which I ever flee?
O vanished joy! O love, that art no more,
  Let my vexed spirit be!

O violet! thy odor through my brain
  Hath searched, and stung to grief
This sunny day, as if a curse did stain
  Thy velvet leaf.

AMELIA B. COPPUCK WELBY

70   *The Old Maid*

WHY sits she thus in solitude? Her heart
    Seems melting in her eyes' delicious blue;
And as it heaves, her ripe lips lie apart,
    As if to let its heavy throbbings through;
In her dark eye a depth of softness swells,
    Deeper than that her careless girlhood wore;
And her cheek crimsons with the hue that tells
    The rich, fair fruit is ripened to the core.

It is her thirtieth birthday! With a sigh
    Her soul hath turned from youth's luxuriant
        bowers,
And her heart taken up the last sweet tie
    That measured out its links of golden hours!
She feels her inmost soul within her stir
    With thoughts too wild and passionate to
        speak;

Yet her full heart — its own interpreter —
   Translates itself in silence on her cheek.

Joy's opening buds, affection's glowing flowers,
   Once lightly sprang within her beaming track ;
O, life was beautiful in those lost hours,
   And yet she does not wish to wander back !
No ! she but loves in loneliness to think
   On pleasures past, though nevermore to be ;
Hope links her to the future, — but the link
   That binds her to the past is memory.

ALICE CARY

71

Pictures of Memory

AMONG the beautiful pictures
  That hang on Memory's wall
Is one of a dim old forest,
  That seemeth best of all;
Not for its gnarled oaks olden,
  Dark with the mistletoe;
Not for the violets golden
  That sprinkle the vale below;
Not for the milk-white lilies
  That lean from the fragrant ledge,
Coquetting all day with the sunbeams,
  And stealing their golden edge;
Not for the vines on the upland,
  Where the bright red berries rest,
Nor the pinks, nor the pale sweet cowslip,
  It seemeth to me the best.

I once had a little brother,
  With eyes that were dark and deep;

In the lap of that old dim forest
   He lieth in peace asleep:
Light as the down of the thistle,
   Free as the winds that blow,
We roved there the beautiful summers,
   The summers of long ago;
But his feet on the hills grew weary,
   And, one of the autumn eves,
I made for my little brother
   A bed of the yellow leaves.
Sweetly his pale arms folded
   My neck in a meek embrace,
As the light of immortal beauty
   Silently covered his face;
And when the arrows of sunset
   Lodged in the tree-tops bright,
He fell, in his saint-like beauty,
   Asleep by the gates of light.
Therefore, of all the pictures
   That hang on Memory's wall,
The one of the dim old forest
   Seemeth the best of all.

PHŒBE CARY

72

Nearer Home

ONE sweetly solemn thought
　　Comes to me o'er and o'er, —
I am nearer home to-day
　　Than I ever have been before; —

Nearer my Father's house
　　Where the many mansions be;
Nearer the great white throne,
　　Nearer the jasper sea; —

Nearer the bound of life
　　Where we lay our burdens down;
Nearer leaving the cross,
　　Nearer gaining the crown.

But lying darkly between,
　　Winding down through the night,
Is the dim and unknown stream
　　That leads at last to the light.

Closer and closer my steps
   Come to the dark abysm;
Closer Death to my lips
   Presses the awful chrysm.

Father, perfect my trust;
   Strengthen the might of my faith;
Let me feel as I would when I stand
   On the rock of the shore of Death,

Feel as I would when my feet
   Are slipping o'er the brink;
For it may be I'm nearer home, —
   Nearer now than I think.

THOMAS BUCHANAN READ

73

Drifting

My soul to-day
Is far away,
Sailing the Vesuvian Bay;
My wingèd boat,
A bird afloat,
Swims round the purple peaks remote

Round purple peaks
It sails, and seeks
Blue inlets and their crystal creeks,
Where high rocks throw,
Through deeps below,
A duplicated golden glow.

Far, vague, and dim
The mountains swim;
While, on Vesuvius' misty brim,

With outstretched hands,
The gray smoke stands
O'erlooking the volcanic lands.

Here Ischia smiles
O'er liquid miles;
And yonder, bluest of the isles,
Calm Capri waits,
Her sapphire gates
Beguiling to her bright estates.

I heed not, if
My rippling skiff
Float swift or slow from cliff to cliff;
With dreamful eyes
My spirit lies
Under the walls of Paradise.

Under the walls
Where swells and falls
The Bay's deep breast at intervals,
At peace I lie,
Blown softly by,
A cloud upon this liquid sky.

The day, so mild,
Is Heaven's own child,
With Earth and Ocean reconciled; —
The airs I feel
Around me steal
Are murmuring to the murmuring keel

Over the rail
My hand I trail
Within the shadow of the sail;
A joy intense,
The cooling sense
Glides down my drowsy indolence.

With dreamful eyes
My spirit lies
Where Summer sings and never dies, —
O'erveiled with vines,
She glows and shines
Among her future oil and wines.

Her children, hid
The cliffs amid,
Are gambolling with the gambolling kid;

Or down the walls,
With tipsy calls,
Laugh on the rocks like waterfalls.

The fisher's child,
With tresses wild,
Unto the smooth, bright sand beguiled,
With glowing lips
Sings as she skips,
Or gazes at the far-off ships.

Yon deep bark goes
Where Traffic blows,
From lands of sun to lands of snows; —
This happier one,
Its course is run
From lands of snow to lands of sun.

O happy ship,
To rise and dip,
With the blue crystal at your lip!
O happy crew,
My heart with you
Sails, and sails, and sings anew

No more, no more
The worldly shore
Upbraids me with its loud uproar!
With dreamful eyes
My spirit lies
Under the walls of Paradise!

In lofty lines,
Mid palms and pines,
And olives, aloes, elms, and vines,
Sorrento swings
On sunset wings,
Where Tasso's spirit soars and sings.

74   *Sheridan's Ride*

Up from the South at break of day,
Bringing to Winchester fresh dismay,
The affrighted air with a shudder bore,
Like a herald in haste, to the chieftain's door,
The terrible grumble and rumble and roar,
Telling the battle was on once more,
And Sheridan twenty miles away.

And wider still those billows of war
Thundered along the horizon's bar;
And louder yet into Winchester rolled
The roar of that red sea uncontrolled,
Making the blood of the listener cold
As he thought of the stake in that fiery fray,
With Sheridan twenty miles away.

But there is a road from Winchester town,
A good, broad highway, leading down;
And there, through the flash of the morning light
A steed as black as the steeds of night
Was seen to pass as with eagle flight.
As if he knew the terrible need,
He stretched away with the utmost speed;
Hills rose and fell, — but his heart was gay.
With Sheridan fifteen miles away.

Still sprung from those swift hoofs, thundering
        South,
The dust, like smoke from the cannon's mouth;
Or the trail of a comet, sweeping faster and faster,
Foreboding to traitors the doom of disaster.
The heart of the steed and the heart of the master

Were beating, like prisoners assaulting their
    walls,
Impatient to be where the battle-field calls;
Every nerve of the charger was strained to full
    play,
With Sheridan only ten miles away.

Under his spurning feet, the road
Like an arrowy Alpine river flowed,
And the landscape sped away behind,
Like an ocean flying before the wind;
And the steed, like a bark fed with furnace ire
Swept on, with his wild eyes full of fire;
But, lo! he is nearing his heart's desire,
He is snuffing the smoke of the roaring fray,
With Sheridan only five miles away.

The first that the General saw were the groups
Of stragglers, and then the retreating troops;
What was done, — what to do, — a glance told
    him both,
And, striking his spurs with a terrible oath,
He dashed down the line mid a storm of huzzas,

And the wave of retreat checked its course there,
    because
The sight of the master compelled it to pause.
With foam and with dust the black charger was
    gray;
By the flash of his eye, and his nostrils' play,
He seemed to the whole great army to say,
"I have brought you Sheridan all the way
From Winchester down, to save the day!"

Hurrah, hurrah for Sheridan!
Hurrah, hurrah for horse and man!
And when their statues are placed on high,
Under the dome of the Union sky, —
The American soldier's Temple of Fame, —
There with the glorious General's name
Be it said in letters both bold and bright:
"Here is the steed that saved the day
By carrying Sheridan into the fight,
From Winchester, — twenty miles away!"

GEORGE HENRY BOKER

75

The Black Regiment

[May 27, 1863.]

DARK as the clouds of even,
Ranked in the western heaven,
Waiting the breath that lifts
All the dead mass, and drifts
Tempest and falling brand
Over a ruined land, —
So still and orderly,
Arm to arm, knee to knee,
Waiting the great event,
Stands the black regiment.

Down the long dusky line
Teeth gleam and eyeballs shine;
And the bright bayonet,
Bristling and firmly set,
Flashed with a purpose grand,

Long ere the sharp command
Of the fierce rolling drum
Told them their time had come,
Told them what work was sent
For the black regiment.

" Now," the flag-sergeant cried,
" Though death and hell betide,
Let the whole nation see
If we are fit to be
Free in this land ; or bound
Down, like the whining hound, —
Bound with red stripes of pain
In our cold chains again ! "
O, what a shout there went
From the black regiment !

"Charge!" Trump and drum awoke;
Onward the bondmen broke ;
Bayonet and sabre-stroke
Vainly opposed their rush.
Through the wild battle's crush,
With but one thought aflush,
Driving their lords like chaff,

In the guns' mouths they laugh;
Or at the slippery brands
Leaping with open hands,
Down they tear man and horse,
Down in their awful course;
Trampling with bloody heel
Over the crashing steel, —
All their eyes forward bent,
Rushed the black regiment.

"Freedom!" their battle-cry, —
"Freedom! or leave to die!"
Ah! and they meant the word,
Not as with us 'tis heard,
Not a mere party shout;
They gave their spirits out,
Trusted the end to God,
And on the gory sod
Rolled in triumphant blood.
Glad to strike one free blow,
Whether for weal or woe;
Glad to breathe one free breath,
Though on the lips of death;

Praying, — alas! in vain! —
That they might fall again,
So they could once more see
That burst to liberty!
This was what "freedom" lent
To the black regiment.

Hundreds on hundreds fell;
But they are resting well;
Scourges and shackles strong
Never shall do them wrong.
O, to the living few,
Soldiers, be just and true!
Hail them as comrades tried;
Fight with them side by side;
Never, in field or tent,
Scorn the black regiment!

BAYARD TAYLOR

76

Bedouin Love-Song

FROM the Desert I come to thee,
  On a stallion shod with fire;
And the winds are left behind
  In the speed of my desire.
Under thy window I stand,
  And the midnight hears my cry:
I love thee, I love but thee!
  With a love that shall not die
    Till the sun grows cold,
    And the stars are old,
    And the leaves of the Judgment
      Book unfold!

Look from thy window, and see
  My passion and my pain!
I lie on the sands below,
  And I faint in thy disdain.

Let the night-winds touch thy brow
  With the heat of my burning sigh,
And melt thee to hear the vow
  Of a love that shall not die
    Till the sun grows cold,
    And the stars are old,
    And the leaves of the Judgment
      Book unfold!

My steps are nightly driven,
  By the fever in my breast,
To hear from thy lattice breathed
  The word that shall give me rest.
Open the door of thy heart,
  And open thy chamber door,
And my kisses shall teach thy lips
  The love that shall fade no more
    Till the sun grows cold
    And the stars are old,
    And the leaves of the Judgment
      Book unfold!

77   *The Arab to the Palm*

NEXT to thee, O fair gazelle,
O Beddowee girl, beloved so well;

Next to the fearless Nedjidee,
Whose fleetness shall bear me again to thee;

Next to ye both, I love the palm,
With his leaves of beauty, his fruit of balm:

Next to ye both, I love the tree
Whose fluttering shadow wraps us three
With love and silence and mystery!

Our tribe is many, our poets vie
With any under the Arab sky;
Yet none can sing of the palm but I.

The marble minarets that begem
Cairo's citadel-diadem
Are not so light as his slender stem.

He lifts his leaves in the sunbeam's glance,
As the Almehs lift their arms in dance, —

A slumberous motion, a passionate sign,
That works in the cells of the blood like wine.

Full of passion and sorrow is he,
Dreaming where the beloved may be;

And when the warm south-winds arise,
He breathes his longing in fervid sighs,

Quickening odors, kisses of balm.
That drop in the lap of his chosen palm.

The sun may flame, and the sands may stir
But the breath of his passion reaches her.

O tree of love, by that love of thine,
Teach me how I shall soften mine!

Give me the secret of the sun,
Whereby the wooed is ever won!

If I were a king, O stately tree,
A likeness, glorious as might be,
In the court of my palace I'd build for thee;

With a shaft of silver, burnished bright,
And leaves of beryl and malachite;

With spikes of golden bloom ablaze,
And fruits of topaz and chrysoprase;

And there the poets, in thy praise,
Should night and morning frame new lays, —

New measures, sung to tunes divine;
But none, O paim, should equal mine!

ETHELINDA ELLIOTT BEERS

All Quiet along the Potomac

"ALL quiet along the Potomac," they say,
    "Except now and then a stray picket
Is shot, as he walks on his beat to and fro,
    By a rifleman hid in the thicket.
'Tis nothing — a private or two now and then
    Will not count in the news of the battle;
Not an officer lost — only one of the men,
    Moaning out, all alone, the death-rattle."

All quiet along the Potomac to-night,
    Where the soldiers lie peacefully dreaming;
Their tents in the rays of the clear autumn
        moon,
    Or the light of the watch-fire, are gleaming.
A tremulous sigh of the gentle night-wind
    Through the forest leaves softly is creeping;

While stars up above, with their glittering
    eyes,
  Keep guard, for the army is sleeping.

There's only the sound of the lone sentry's
    tread,
  As he tramps from the rock to the fountain,
And thinks of the two in the low trundle-bed
  Far away in the cot on the mountain.
His musket falls slack; his face, dark and
    grim,
  Grows gentle with memories tender,
As he mutters a prayer for the children asleep,
  For their mother; may Heaven defend her!

The moon seems to shine just as brightly as
    then,
That night, when the love yet unspoken
Leaped up to his lips — when low-murmured
    vows
  Were pledged to be ever unbroken.
Then drawing his sleeve roughly over his eyes.
  He dashes off tears that are welling,

And gathers his gun closer up to its place,
  As if to keep down the heart-swelling.

He passes the fountain, the blasted pine-tree,
  The footstep is lagging and weary;
Yet onward he goes, through the broad belt of
    light,
  Toward the shade of the forest so dreary.
Hark! was it the night-wind that rustled the
    leaves?
  Was it moonlight so wondrously flashing?
It looked like a rifle . . . "Ha! Mary, good-
    by!"
  The red life-blood is ebbing and plashing.

All quiet along the Potomac to-night;
  No sound save the rush of the river;
While soft falls the dew on the face of the
    dead —
  The picket's off duty forever!

WILLIAM HAINES LYTLE

79   *Antony to Cleopatra*

"I am dying, Egypt, dying." — SHAKESPEARE'S
Antony and Cleopatra, Act iv. Sc. 13

I AM dying, Egypt, dying,
  Ebbs the crimson life-tide fast,
And the dark Plutonian shadows
  Gather on the evening blast;
Let thine arms, O Queen, enfold me,
  Hush thy sobs and bow thine ear;
Listen to the great heart-secrets,
  Thou, and thou alone, must hear.

Though my scarred and veteran legions
  Bear their eagles high no more,
And my wrecked and scattered galleys
  Strew dark Actium's fatal shore,
Though no glittering guards surround me,
  Prompt to do their master's will,

I must perish like a Roman,
  Die the great Triumvir still.

Let not Cæsar's servile minions
  Mock the lion thus laid low;
'Twas no foeman's arm that felled **him,**
  'Twas his own that struck the blow:
His who, pillowed on thy bosom,
  Turned aside from glory's ray,
His who, drunk with thy caresses,
  Madly threw a world away.

Should the base plebeian rabble
  Dare assail my name at Rome,
Where my noble spouse, Octavia,
  Weeps within her widowed home,
Seek her; say the gods bear witness —
  Altars, augurs, circling wings —
That her blood, with mine commingled,
  Yet shall mount the throne of kings.

As for thee, star-eyed Egyptian!
  Glorious sorceress of the Nile!

Light the path to Stygian horrors
　　With the splendors of thy smile.
Give the Cæsar crowns and arches,
　　Let his brow the laurel twine;
I can scorn the Senate's triumphs,
　　Triumphing in love like thine.

I am dying, Egypt, dying!
　　Hark! the insulting foeman's cry.
They are coming — quick, my falchion!
　　Let me front them ere I die.
Ah! no more amid the battle
　　Shall my heart exulting swell;
Isis and Osiris guard thee!
　　Cleopatra — Rome — farewell!

ROSE TERRY COOKE

Rêve du Midi

WHEN o'er the mountain steeps
The hazy noontide creeps,
And the shrill cricket sleeps
    Under the grass ;
When soft the shadows lie,
And clouds sail o'er the sky,
And the idle winds go by,
With the heavy scent of blossoms as they
    pass, —

Then, when the silent stream
Lapses as in a dream,
And the water-lilies gleam
    Up to the sun ;
When the hot and burdened day
Rests on its downward way,
When the moth forgets to play,
And the plodding ant may dream her work is
    done, —

Then, from the noise of war
And the din of earth afar,
Like some forgotten star
          Dropt from the sky, —
The sounds of love and fear,
All voices sad and clear,
Banished to silence drear, —
The willing thrall of trances sweet I lie.

Some melancholy gale
Breathes its mysterious tale,
Till the rose's lips grow pale
          With her sighs;
And o'er my thoughts are cast
Tints of the vanished past,
Glories that faded fast,
Renewed to splendor in my dreaming eyes.

As poised on vibrant wings,
Where its sweet treasure swings,
The honey-lover clings
          To the red flowers, —

So, lost in vivid light,
So, rapt from day and night,
I linger in delight,
Enraptured o'er the vision-freighted hours.

RICHARD HENRY STODDARD

81

It Never Comes Again

THERE are gains for all our losses,
    There are balms for all our pain,
But when youth, the dream, departs
It takes something from our hearts,
    And it never comes again.

We are stronger, and are better,
    Under manhood's sterner reign;
Still we feel that something sweet
Followed youth, with flying feet,
    And will never come again.

Something beautiful is vanished,
    And we sigh for it in vain;
We behold it everywhere,
On the earth, and in the air,
    But it never comes again.

82   *The Sea*

Through the night, through the night,
  In the saddest unrest,
Wrapt in white, all in white,
  With her babe on her breast,
Walks the mother so pale,
Staring out on the gale,
  Through the night.

Through the night, through the night
  Where the sea lifts the wreck,
Land in sight, close in sight,
  On the surf-flooded deck,
Stands the father so brave,
Driving on to his grave,
  Through the night.

COATES KINNEY

Rain on the Roof

WHEN the humid shadows hover
    Over all the starry spheres,
And the melancholy darkness
    Gently weeps in rainy tears,
What a bliss to press the pillow
    Of a cottage-chamber bed,
And to listen to the patter
    Of the soft rain overhead!

Every tinkle on the shingles
    Has an echo in the heart;
And a thousand dreamy fancies
    Into busy being start,
And a thousand recollections
    Weave their air-threads into woof,
As I listen to the patter
    Of the rain upon the roof.

Now in memory comes my mother,
    As she used, in years agone,
To regard the darling dreamers
    Ere she left them till the dawn:
O! I see her leaning o'er me,
    As I list to this refrain
Which is played upon the shingles
    By the patter of the rain.

Then my little seraph sister,
    With the wings and waving hair,
And her star-eyed cherub brother —
    A serene angelic pair! —
Glide around my wakeful pillow,
    With their praise or mild reproof,
As I listen to the murmur
    Of the soft rain on the roof.

And another comes, to thrill me
    With her eyes' delicious blue;
And I mind not, musing on her,
    That her heart was all untrue:
I remember but to love her
    With a passion kin to pain,

And my heart's quick pulses vibrate
　　To the patter of the rain.

Art hath naught of tone or cadence
　　That can work with such a spell
In the soul's mysterious fountains,
　　Whence the tears of rapture well,
As that melody of nature,
　　That subdued, subduing strain
Which is played upon the shingles
　　By the patter of the rain.

HENRY TIMROD

84   *Dreams*

Who first said "False as dreams"? Not one
    who saw
    Into the wild and wondrous world they sway;
No thinker who hath read their mystic law;
    No poet who hath weaved them in his lay.

Else had he known that through the human
    breast
    Cross and recross a thousand fleeting gleams,
That, passed unnoticed in the day's unrest,
    Come out at night, like stars, in shining
        dreams;

That minds too busy or too dull to mark
    The dim suggestion of the noisier hours,
By dreams in the deep silence of the dark
    Are roused at midnight with their folded
        powers.

Like that old fount beneath Dodona's oaks,
    That, dry and voiceless in the garish noon,
When the calm night arose with modest looks,
    Caught with full wave the sparkle of the moon.

If, now and then, a ghastly shape glide in,
    And fright us with its horrid gloom or glee,
It is the ghost of some forgotten sin
    We failed to exorcise on bended knee.

And that sweet face which only yesternight
    Came to thy solace, dreamer (didst thou read
The blessing in its eyes of tearful light?),
    Was but the spirit of some gentle deed.

Each has its lesson; for our dreams in sooth,
    Come they in shape of demons, gods, or elves
Are allegories with deep hearts of truth
    That tell us solemn secrets of ourselves.

GUY HUMPHREY McMASTER

85

Carmen Bellicosum

IN their ragged regimentals
Stood the old Continentals,
          Yielding not,
When the grenadiers were lunging,
And like hail fell the plunging
          Cannon-shot;
          When the files
          Of the isles,
From the smoky night encampment, bore the
     banner of the rampant
          Unicorn,
And grummer, grummer, grummer rolled the roll
     of the drummer,
          Through the morn!

Then with eyes to the front all,
And with guns horizontal,
          Stood our sires;

And the balls whistled deadly,
And in streams flashing redly
    Blazed the fires;
    As the roar
    On the shore,
Swept the strong battle-breakers o'er the green
    sodded acres
    Of the plain;
And louder, louder, louder, cracked the black
    gunpowder,
    Cracking amain!

Now like smiths at their forges
Worked the red St. George's
    Cannoneers;
And the "villanous saltpetre"
Rung a fierce, discordant metre
    Round their ears;
    As the swift
    Storm-drift,
With hot sweeping anger, came the horseguards'
    clangor,
    On our flanks;

Then higher, higher, higher, burned the old-
   fashioned fire
         Through the ranks!

      Then the bare-headed colonel
      Galloped through the white infernal
         Powder-cloud;
      And his broadsword was swinging,
      And his brazen throat was ringing
         Trumpet-loud.
      Then the blue
      Bullets flew,
And the trooper-jackets redden at the touch of
   the leaden
         Rifle-breath;
And rounder, rounder, rounder, roared the iron
   six-pounder,
         Hurling death!

PAUL HAMILTON HAYNE

86

Preëxistence

WHILE sauntering through the crowded street,
Some half-remembered face I meet,

Albeit upon no mortal shore
That face, methinks, has smiled before.

Lost in a gay and festal throng,
I tremble at some tender song, —

Set to an air whose golden bars
I must have heard in other stars.

In sacred aisles I pause to share
The blessings of a priestly prayer, —

When the whole scene which greets mine eyes
In some strange mode I recognize

As one whose every mystic part
I feel prefigured in my heart.

At sunset, as I calmly stand,
A stranger on an alien strand,

Familiar as my childhood's home
Seems the long stretch of wave and foam.

One sails toward me o'er the bay,
And what he comes to do and say

I can foretell.   A prescient lore
Springs from some life outlived of yore.

O swift, instinctive, startling gleams
Of deep soul-knowledge! not as *dreams*

For aye ye vaguely dawn and die,
But oft with lightning certainty

Pierce through the dark, oblivious brain,
To make old thoughts and memories plain,

Thoughts which perchance must travel back
Across the wild, bewildering track

Of countless æons; memories far,
High-reaching as yon pallid star,

Unknown, scarce seen, whose flickering grace
Faints on the outmost rings of space!

87   *In Harbor*

I THINK it is over, over,
    I think it is over at last:
Voices of foemen and lover,
    The sweet and the bitter have passed:
Life, like a tempest of ocean,
    Hath outblown its ultimate blast:
There's but a faint sobbing seaward,
While the calm of the tide deepens leeward,
And behold! like the welcoming quiver
Of heart-pulses throbbed through the river,
    Those lights in the harbor at last,
    The heavenly harbor at last!

I feel it is over! over!
    For the winds and the waters surcease;
Ah, few were the days of the rover
    That smiled in the beauty of peace,
And distant and dim was the omen
    That hinted redress or release!
From the ravage of life, and its riot,
What marvel I yearn for the quiet
    Which bides in the harbor at last, —

For the lights, with their welcoming quiver
That throbs through the sanctified river,
  Which girdle the harbor at last,
  This heavenly harbor at last?

I know it is over, over,
  I know it is over at last!
Down sail! the sheathed anchor uncover,
For the stress of the voyage has passed:
Life, like a tempest of ocean,
  Hath outbreathed its ultimate blast:
There's but a faint sobbing seaward,
While the calm of the tide deepens leeward;
And behold! like the welcoming quiver
Of heart-pulses throbbed through the river,
  Those lights in the harbor at last,
  The heavenly harbor at last!

EMILY DICKINSON

88 *I Never Saw a Moor*

I NEVER saw a moor,
I never saw the sea;
Yet know I how the heather looks,
And what a wave must be.

I never spoke with God,
Nor visited in heaven;
Yet certain am I of the spot
As if the chart were given.

89 *Indian Summer*

THESE are the days when birds come back,
A very few, a bird or two,
To take a backward look.

These are the days when skies put on
The old, old sophistries of June,—
A blue and gold mistake.

Oh, fraud that cannot cheat the bee,
Almost thy plausibility
Induces my belief,

Till ranks of seeds their witness bear,
And softly through the altered air
Hurries a timid leaf!

Oh, sacrament of summer days,
Oh, last communion in the haze,
Permit a child to join,

Thy sacred emblems to partake,
Thy consecrated bread to break,
Taste thine immortal wine!

HELEN HUNT JACKSON

Habeas Corpus

My body, eh?   Friend Death, how now?
   Why all this tedious pomp of writ?
Thou hast reclaimed it sure and slow
   For half a century, bit by bit.

In faith thou knowest more to-day
   Than I do, where it can be found!
This shrivelled lump of suffering clay,
   To which I now am chained and bound,

Has not of kith or kin a trace
   To the good body once I bore;
Look at this shrunken, ghastly face:
   Didst ever see that face before?

Ah, well, friend Death, good friend thou art;
   Thy only fault thy lagging gait,
Mistaken pity in thy heart
   For timorous ones that bid thee wait.

Do quickly all thou hast to do,
  Nor I nor mine will hindrance make;
I shall be free when thou art through;
  I grudge thee naught that thou must take!

Stay! I have lied: I grudge thee one,
  Yes, two I grudge thee at this last, —
Two members which have faithful done
  My will and bidding in the past.

I grudge thee this right hand of mine;
  I grudge thee this quick-beating heart;
They never gave me coward sign,
  Nor played me once a traitor's part.

I see now why in olden days
  Men in barbaric love or hate
Nailed enemies' hands at wild crossways,
  Shrined leaders' hearts in costly state:

The symbol, sign, and instrument
  Of each soul's purpose, passion, strife,
Of fires in which are poured and spent
  Their all of love, their all of life.

O feeble, mighty human hand !
  O fragile, dauntless human heart !
The universe holds nothing planned
  With such sublime, transcendent art !

Yes, Death, I own I grudge thee mine
  Poor little hand, so feeble now ;
Its wrinkled palm, its altered line,
  Its veins so pallid and so slow —

[*Unfinished here.*]

Ah, well, friend Death, good friend thou art ;
  I shall be free when thou art through
Take all there is — take hand and heart :
  There must be somewhere work to do.

Her last poem: August 7, 1885.

MARY WOOLSEY HOWLAND

91

Rest

I LAY me down to sleep,
    With little care
Whether my waking find
    Me here, or there.

A bowing, burdened head
    That only asks to rest,
Unquestioning, upon
    A loving breast.

My good right hand forgets
    Its cunning now;
To march the weary march
    I know not how.

I am not eager, bold,
    Nor strong, — all that is past;

I am ready not to do,
    At last, at last.

My half-day's work is done,
    And this is all my part, —
I give a patient God
    My patient heart;

And grasp his banner still,
    Though all the blue be dim;
These stripes as well as stars
    Lead after him.

JOHN JAMES INGALLS

92

Opportunity

" MASTER of human destinies am I!
Fame, love, and fortune on my footsteps wait.
Cities and fields I walk; I penetrate
Deserts and seas remote, and passing by
Hovel and mart and palace — soon or late
I knock unbidden once at every gate!

" If sleeping, wake — if feasting, rise before
I turn away.   It is the hour of fate,
And they who follow me reach every state
Mortals desire, and conquer every foe
Save death; but those who doubt or hesitate,
Condemned to failure, penury, and woe,
Seek me in vain and uselessly implore.
I answer not, and I return no more!"

GEORGE ARNOLD

93   *September*

SWEET is the voice that calls
From babbling waterfalls
In meadows where the downy seeds are flying;
And soft the breezes blow,
And eddying come and go
In faded gardens where the rose is dying.

Among the stubbled corn
The blithe quail pipes at morn,
The merry partridge drums in hidden places,
And glittering insects gleam
Above the reedy stream,
Where busy spiders spin their filmy laces.

At eve, cool shadows fall
Across the garden wall,
And on the clustered grapes to purple turning;

And pearly vapors lie
Along the eastern sky,
Where the broad harvest-moon is redly burning.

Ah, soon on field and hill
The wind shall whistle chill,
And patriarch swallows call their flocks together,
To fly from frost and snow,
And seek for lands where blow
The fairer blossoms of a balmier weather.

The cricket chirps all day,
"O fairest summer, stay!"
The squirrel eyes askance the chestnuts brown-
ing;
The wild fowl fly afar
Above the foamy bar,
And hasten southward ere the skies are frown
ing.

Now comes a fragrant breeze
Through the dark cedar-trees,
And round about my temples fondly lingers,

In gentle playfulness,
Like to the soft caress.
Bestowed in happier days by loving fingers.

Yet, though a sense of grief
Comes with the falling leaf,
And memory makes the summer doubly pleasant,
In all my autumn dreams
A future summer gleams,
Passing the fairest glories of the present!

HENRY AMES BLOOD

94

The Song of the Savoyards

FAR poured past Broadway's lamps alight
  The tumult of her motley throng,
When high and clear upon the night
  Rose an inspiring song,
And rang above the city's din
To sound of harp and violin;
  A simple but a manly strain,
  And ending with the brave refrain —
Courage! Courage, mon camarade!

And now, where rose that song of cheer,
  Both young and old stood still for joy;
Or from the windows hung to hear
  The children of Savoy:
And many an eye with rapture glowed,
And saddest hearts forgot their load,
  And feeble souls grew strong again,
  So stirring was the brave refrain —
Courage! Courage, mon camarade!

Alone, with only silence there,
   Awaiting his life's welcome close,
A sick man lay, when on the air
   That clarion arose;
So sweet the thrilling cadence rang,
It seemed to him an angel sang,
   And sang to him; and he would fain
   Have died upon that heavenly strain —
Courage ! Courage, mon camarade !

A sorrow-stricken man and wife,
   With nothing left them but to pray,
Heard streaming over their sad life
   That grand, heroic lay:
And through the mist of happy tears
They saw the promise-laden years;
   And in their joy they sang again
   And carolled high the fond refrain —
Courage ! Courage, mon camarade !

Two artists, in the cloud of gloom
   Which hung upon their hopes deferred,
Resounding through their garret-room
   That noble chanson heard;

And, as the night before the day,
Their weak misgivings fled away;
    And with the burden of the strain
    They made their studio ring again —
Courage! Courage, mon camarade!

Two poets who in patience wrought
    The glory of an aftertime, —
Lords of an age which knew them **not**,
    Heard rise that lofty rhyme;
And on their hearts it fell, as falls
The sunshine upon prison walls;
    And one caught up the magic strain
    And to the other sang again —
Courage! Courage, mon camarade!

And unto one, who, tired of breath
    And day and night and name and **fame,**
Held to his lips a glass of death,
    That song a saviour came;
Beseeching him from his despair,
As with the passion of a prayer;

And kindling in his heart and brain
  The valor of its blest refrain —
Courage!   Courage, mon camarade!

O thou, with earthly ills beset,
  Call to thy lips those words of joy,
And never in thy life forget
  The brave song of Savoy!
For those dear words may have the power
To cheer thee in thy darkest hour;
  The memory of that loved refrain
  Bring gladness to thy heart again! —
Courage!   Courage, mon camarade!

ABRAM JOSEPH RYAN

95

Sentinel Songs [1]

WHEN falls the soldier brave
  Dead — at the feet of wrong, —
The poet sings, and guards his grave
  With sentinels of song.

Songs, march! he gives command,
  Keep faithful watch and true;
The living and dead of the Conquered Land
  Have now no guards save you.

Grave Ballads! mark ye well!
  Thrice holy is your trust!
Go! halt! by the fields where warriors fell,
  Rest arms! and guard their dust.

List, Songs! your watch is long!
  The soldiers' guard was brief,

[1] Selected from "Father Ryan's Poems," published by P. J. Kenedy, New York. Copyrighted.

Whilst right is right, and wrong is wrong,
    Ye may not seek relief.

Go! wearing the gray of grief!
    Go! watch o'er the Dead in Gray!
Go guard the private and guard the chief,
    And sentinel their clay!

And the songs, in stately rhyme,
    And with softly sounding tread,
Go forth, to watch for a time — a time,
    Where sleep the Deathless Dead.

And the songs, like funeral dirge,
    In music soft and low,
Sing round the graves, — whilst hot tears arge
    From hearts that are homes of woe.

What though no sculptured shaft
    Immortalize each brave?
What though no monument epitaphed
    Be built above each grave?

When marble wears away,
    And monuments are dust, —

The songs that guard our soldiers' clay
　　Will still fulfil their trust.

With lifted head, and steady tread,
　　Like stars that guard the skies,
Go watch each bed, where rest the dead,
　　Brave Songs! with sleepless eyes.

SIDNEY LANIER

96

Song of the Chattahoochee

OUT of the hills of Habersham,
Down the valleys of Hall,
I hurry amain to reach the plain,
Run the rapid and leap the fall,
Split at the rock and together again,
Accept my bed, or narrow or wide,
And flee from folly on every side
With a lover's pain to attain the plain
  Far from the hills of Habersham,
  Far from the valleys of Hall.

All down the hills of Habersham,
  All through the valleys of Hall,
The rushes cried *Abide, abide,*
The wilful waterweeds held me thrall,
The loving laurel turned my tide,
The ferns and the fondling grass said *Stay.*

The dewberry dipped for to work delay,
And the little reeds sighed *Abide, abide,*
   Here in the hills of Habersham,
   Here in the valleys of Hall.

   High o'er the hills of Habersham,
     Veiling the valleys of Hall,
The hickory told me manifold
Fair tales of shade; the poplar tall
Wrought me her shadowy self to hold;
The chestnut, the oak, the walnut, the pine,
Overleaning, with flickering meaning and sign,
Said, *Pass not, so cold, these manifold*
   Deep shades of the hills of Habersham,
   These glades in the valleys of Hall.

   And oft in the hills of Habersham,
     And oft in the valleys of Hall,
The white quartz shone, and the smooth brook
    stone
Did bar me of passage with friendly brawl;
And many a luminous jewel alone
— Crystal clear or a-cloud with mist,

Ruby, or garnet, or amethyst —
Made lures with the lights of streaming **stone**
 In the clefts of the hills of Habersham,
 In the beds of the valleys of Hall.

 But oh! not the hills of Habersham,
 And oh! not the valleys of Hall
Avail; I am fain for to water the plain.
Downward the voices of Duty call;
Downward to toil and be mixed with the **main,**
The dry fields burn, and the mills are to turn,
And a myriad flowers mortally yearn,
And the lordly main from beyond the **plain**
 Calls o'er the hills of Habersham,
 Calls through the valleys of Hall.

97 *A Ballad of Trees and the Master*

INTO the woods my Master went,
Clean forspent, forspent.
Into the woods my Master came,
Forspent with love and shame.
But the olives they were not blind to Him;
The little gray leaves were kind to Him;

The thorn-tree had a mind to Him
When into the woods he came.

Out of the woods my Master went,
And He was well content.
Out of the woods my Master came,
Content with death and shame.
When Death and Shame would woo Him last,
From under the trees they drew Him last:
'Twas on a tree they slew Him — last,
When out of the woods He came.

JOHN HENRY BONER

98

Poe's Cottage at Fordham

Here lived the soul enchanted
  By melody of song;
Here dwelt the spirit haunted
  By a demoniac throng;
Here sang the lips elated;
Here grief and death were sated;
Here loved and here unmated
  Was he, so frail, so strong.

Here wintry winds and cheerless
  The dying firelight blew,
While he whose song was peerless
  Dreamed the drear midnight through
And from dull embers chilling
Crept shadows darkly filling
The silent place, and thrilling
  His fancy as they grew.

Here, with brow bared to heaven,
    In starry night he stood,
With the lost star of seven
    Feeling sad brotherhood.
Here in the sobbing showers
Of dark autumnal hours
He heard suspected powers
    Shriek through the stormy wood.

From visions of Apollo
    And of Astarte's bliss,
He gazed into the hollow
    And hopeless vale of Dis;
And though earth were surrounded
By heaven, it still was mounded
With graves.   His soul had sounded
    The dolorous abyss.

Proud, mad, but not defiant,
    He touched at heaven and hell.
Fate found a rare soul pliant
    And rung her changes well.

Alternately his lyre,
Stranded with strings of fire,
Led earth's most happy choir,
    Or flashed with Israfel.

No singer of old story
    Luting accustomed lays,
No harper for new glory,
    No mendicant for praise,
He struck high chords and splendid,
Wherein were fiercely blended
Tones that unfinished ended
    With his unfinished days.

Here through this lowly portal,
    Made sacred by his name,
Unheralded immortal
    The mortal went and came.
And fate that then denied him,
And envy that decried him,
And malice that belied him,
    Have cenotaphed his fame.

CAROLINE SPENCER

99

Living Waters

THERE are some hearts like wells, green-mossed
    and deep
  As ever summer saw;
And cool their water is, — yea, cool and sweet; —
  But you must come to draw.
They hoard not, yet they rest in calm content,
  And not unsought will give;
They can be quiet with their wealth unspent,
  So self-contained they live.

And there are some like springs, that bubbling
    burst
  To follow dusty ways,
And run with offered cup to quench his thirst
  Where the tired traveller strays;
That never ask the meadows if they want
  What is their joy to give;

Unasked, their lives to other life they grant,
  So self-bestowed they live!

And One is like the ocean, deep and wide,
  Wherein all waters fall;
That girdles the broad earth, and draws the
    tide,
  Feeding and bearing all;
That breathes the mists, that sends the clouds
    abroad,
  That takes, again to give; —
Even the great and loving heart of God,
  Whereby all love doth live.

RICHARD HOVEY

100 *The Faun*

A FRAGMENT

I WILL go out to grass with that old King,
For I am weary of clothes and cooks.
I long to lie along the banks of brooks,
And watch the boughs above me sway and
    swing.
Come, I will pluck off custom's livery,
Nor longer be a lackey to old Time,
Time shall serve me, and at my feet shall fling
The spoil of listless minutes.   I shall climb
The wild trees for my food, and run
Through dale and upland as the fox runs free,
Laugh for cool joy and sleep i' the warm sun,
And men will call me mad, like that old King.

For I am woodland-natured, and have made
Dryads my bedfellows,
And I have played

With the sleek Naiads in the splash of the pools
And made me mock of gowned and trousered
    fools.
Helen, none knows
Better than thou how like a Faun I strayed.
And I am half Faun now, and my heart goes
Out to the forest and the crack of twigs,
The drip of wet leaves and the low soft laughter
Of brooks that chuckle o'er old mossy jests
And say them over to themselves, the nests
Of squirrels and the holes the chipmunk digs,
Where through the branches the slant rays
Dapple with sunlight the leaf-matted ground,
And the wind comes with blown vestures
    rustling after,
And through the woven lattice of crisp sound
A bird's song lightens like a maiden's face.

O wildwood Helen, let them strive and fret,
Those goggled men with their dissecting-knives!
Let them in charnel-houses pass their lives
And seek in death life's secret! And let
Those hard-faced worldlings prematurely old
Gnaw their thin lips with vain desire to get

Portia's fair fame or Lesbia's carcanet,
Or crown of Cæsar or Catullus,
Apicius' lampreys or Crassus' gold!
For these consider many things — but yet
By land or sea
They shall not find the way to Arcady,
The old home of the awful heart-dear Mother,
Whereto child-dreams and long rememberings
    lull
Far from the cares that overlay and smother
The memories of old woodland out-door mirth
In the dim first life-burst centuries ago,
The sense of the freedom and nearness of
    Earth —
Nay, this they shall not know;
For who goes thither
Leaves all the cark and clutch of his soul behind,
The doves defiled and the serpents shrined,
The hates that wax and the hopes that wither;
Nor does he journey, seeking where it be,
But wakes and finds himself in Arcady.
Hist! there's a stir in the brush.
Was it a face through the leaves?

Back of the laurels a skurry and rush
Hillward, then silence except for the thrush
That throws one song from the dark of the
    bush
And is gone; and I plunge in the wood, and
    the swift soul cleaves
Through the swirl and the flow of the leaves,
As a swimmer stands with his white limbs bare
    to the sun
For the space that a breath is held, and drops in
    the sea;
And the undulant woodland folds round me, in-
    timate, fluctuant, free,
Like the clasp and the cling of the waters, and
    the reach and the effort is done, —
There is only the glory of living, exultant to be.

O goodly damp smell of the ground!
O rough sweet bark of the trees!
O clear sharp cracklings of sound!
O life that's a-thrill and a-bound
With the vigor of boyhood and morning, and
    the noontide's rapture of ease!
Was there ever a weary heart in the world?

A lag in the body's urge or a flag of the spirit's
     wings?
Did a man's heart ever break
For a lost hope's sake?
For here there is lilt in the quiet and calm in
     the quiver of things.
Ay, this old oak, gray-grown and knurled,
Solemn and sturdy and big,
Is as young of heart, as alert and elate in his
     rest,
As the nuthatch there that clings to the tip of
     the twig
And scolds at the wind that buffets too rudely
     its nest.

Oh, what is it breathes in the air?
Oh, what is it touches my cheek?
There's a sense of a presence that lurks in the
     branches.
But where?
Is it far, is it far to seek?

INDEX OF FIRST LINES